LEGENDS OF WARFARE

GROUND

USMC Tracked Amphibious Vehicles

T46E1/M76 Otter, M116 Husky, LVTP5, and LVTP7/AAV7A1

DAVID DOYLE

SCHIFFER MILITARY

4880 Lower Valley Road   Atglen, PA 19310

Designed by Christopher Bower
Cover design by Justin Watkinson
Type set in Impact/Minion Pro/Univers LT Std

ISBN: 978-0-7643-6784-7
Printed in India

Published by Schiffer Publishing, Ltd.
4880 Lower Valley Road
Atglen, PA 19310
Phone: (610) 593-1777; Fax: (610) 593-2002
Email: Info@schifferbooks.com
Web: www.schifferbooks.com

For our complete selection of fine books on this and related subjects, please visit our website at www.schifferbooks.com. You may also write for a free catalog.

Schiffer Publishing's titles are available at special discounts for bulk purchases for sales promotions or premiums. Special editions, including personalized covers, corporate imprints, and excerpts, can be created in large quantities for special needs. For more information, contact the publisher.

We are always looking for people to write books on new and related subjects. If you have an idea for a book, please contact us at proposals@schifferbooks.com.

Acknowledgments

From the time that Donald Roebling conceived what came to be known as the Amphibious Tractor in 1937, the amtracs, as they were abbreviated, have been a key part of the American arsenal. Although they are most often associated with and used by the Marines, the US Army is often involved in the development and procurement of these vehicles, which have been produced in several varieties by multiple firms. This book, which focuses on tracked amphibians, both amtracs and carriers, would not have been possible without the help of several of these organizations and institutions dedicated to archiving these activities. In addition, assembling a book such as this requires a great deal of help from friends and associates.

I would like to personally thank Tom Kailbourn, Scott Taylor, Chun Hsu, Steve Zaloga, Tracy White, Chris Hughes, John Cheney II, Kevin Emdee, the late Dave Harper, and Patrick Tipton for their help with this project.

In addition, I thank the staffs of General Motors LLC, PACCAR Inc., the TACOM LCMC History Office, the Marine Corps History Division, Washington University, the National Archives and Records Administration, the Rock Island Arsenal Museum, and the US Army Ordnance TSF.

Most especially, thanks are due my lovely wife, Denise, who, in addition to accompanying me on innumerable research trips and scanning thousands of documents and photos, has continued to support my writing efforts while all the while shouldering the burden of maintaining our household as I spend countless hours at the keyboard.

All photos not otherwise credited are from the US Department of Defense.

Introduction

Even before the Allied victory in World War II, the US military had begun considering what the next generation of military vehicles would look like, with special emphasis on standardizing as many components as possible across the entire range of vehicles. From engines to comparatively minor items such as instrument panel components, the greater the standardization, the less the logistical burden.

The hard-fought battles on the beaches, both in the Pacific and in Europe, pointed to the need for more-capable amphibious tractors, and while the Weasel was an extremely successful combination of low-ground-pressure vehicle and amphibian, there was a desire for a vehicle with similar abilities, but with greater cargo capacity and improved shelter for the crew.

The vehicles produced as a result of these efforts would see combat in Vietnam, and that experience would lead to further developments, resulting in yet another generation of vehicles that would serve capably in the Gulf War.

In this volume we will examine these vehicles and their use.

Contents

CHAPTER 1

The T46E1/M76 Otter

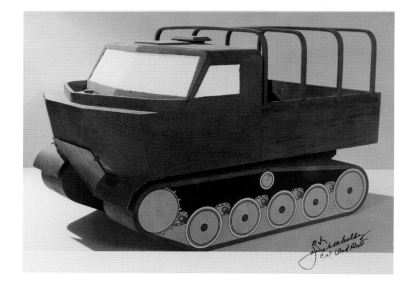

Soon after the end of World War II, the US Army began to consider a new amphibious vehicle that would improve on the M29 Weasel. A key feature would be an enclosed cab, since the open cab of the Weasel was prone to swamping. This photo, dated November 27, 1946, shows a model of a proposed amphibious tracked cargo carrier with an enclosed cab, but with an open cargo compartment with bows for a tarpaulin cover. *Military History Institute*

On August 16, 1945, the Ordnance Committee approved the development of two 1½-ton amphibian cargo carriers, to be designated T37 and T37E1. These vehicles were envisioned as replacements for both the Weasel and the DUKW. However, by October 30, 1947, the Ordnance Committee had reconsidered its position and recommended that two T46 amphibian cargo carriers be built rather than the previously approved T37/T37E1. The specifications of the new vehicle were that it would be

- amphibious
- fully enclosed
- air transportable
- suitable for deep snow
- suitable to transport cargo or personnel

The Automotive Ordnance Group of General Motors responded with a preliminary design and proposal for the T46. General Motors was awarded contract DA-20-089-ORD-1552 to produce a mockup and two pilots, although this was later reduced to a mockup and one pilot. Following inspection of the mockup, the government requested some changes, and a pilot was built. The pilot was powered by a naturally aspirated, four-cylinder, horizontally opposed Continental AO-268-2 air-cooled engine.

Following testing, additional modifications were called for, including, most notably, changes in the suspension, transmission, and propellers. The trailing-arm idler was replaced by a raised idler, the transmission was changed from the CD-150-1 with wobble stick control to the C-150 with handlebar control, and

the dual propellers gave way to a single propeller. The road wheels, previously 6:00-12 pneumatic tires, were now 6.60-15 pneumatic tires, and the track width was increased from 28½ inches to 30 inches. After these changes, the vehicle was redesignated the T46E1. In November 1949 the T46E1 was shipped to Aberdeen Proving Ground for testing and evaluation.

In June 1950, the Pontiac Division of General Motors was awarded a contract to produce six production pilot T46E1 vehicles for troop trials. These vehicles were produced under the direction of Leonard Moore, Dale McCormick, Paul Metzler, and William Killen.

The vehicle hulls were constructed of aluminum alloy riveted to a steel framework. Each side panel from the front door aft was a single sheet of aluminum. The engine, crew, and cargo compartments were separated by bulkheads, and watertight construction was used throughout. The vehicle had a capacity of the driver plus nine men, or 1½ tons of cargo. A large trapezoidal-shaped stack between the driver's and assistant driver's seats was used for engine intake air requirements. The stack also housed the engine and heater exhaust outlets.

Beyond the previously mentioned framework, the only steel used in the construction of the vehicle was small pieces used for reinforcement at equipment attachment points and behind the ladders.

The driver and assistant driver were provided with a door with roll-down windows, and doors were equipped with rubber gaskets, making them watertight. Additionally, above each of these men were drawn aluminum hatches. The assistant driver's hatch could be equipped with a ring mount for an antiaircraft machine gun. The rear cargo area was accessed through a 30-by-30-inch rear door or a 50-by-50-inch roof hatch.

$12,500,000 contract for Army rockets. The other is a $45,000,000 contract for a new type of amphibious cargo carrier for the Army."

The *Free Press* article continued: "[General manager Arnold] Lenz said that approximately 2,000 will work on the carrier project. Extensive tooling for the project is under way. The GM technical development laboratories worked with Army experts for two years experimenting with and building initial models."

While the Army handled the procurement of the Otter, the Marine Corps had been interested in the vehicle essentially from the outset. In fact, Marine Corps major Duensing supervised many of the early 1951 tests.

The 1952 Pontiac Engineering Annual Report provides the company's point of view on the progress of the T46E1, stating:

The vehicle rode on two tracks, each made of three belts, with 176 shoes per track. Each track in turn ran on four pairs of ten-ply pneumatic tires, which were suspended from torsion bars. As a result, the vehicle had a smooth ride and a remarkably low ground pressure of 2.3 pounds per square inch. Hence it could operate over deep snow on which a man could not walk, as well as being able to traverse deep, viscous mud.

On March 16, 1951, contract DA-2-018-ORD-11292 (F), in the amount of $12,000,000.00 was issued to the Pontiac Motor Division by the Detroit Ordnance District. This contract provided for the production of 203 of the T46E1 carriers, as well as the establishment of the necessary facilities to undertake said production. Subsequently, contract DA-20-018-ORD-12205 "undertook to establish a capacity for manufacture of not less than 50 per month on 1 8-hr day, 5 day per week basis and supply 203 carriers in quantities not to exceed 20 per month." The first 60 of these vehicles would cost $202,902.00 each, and thereafter the price would be $58,592.00. The difference in cost was related to the amortization of the cost of start-up production.

Concerning the new vehicle, the March 22, 1951, *Detroit Free Press*, while transposing the dollar amounts, reported that "the Pontiac Motor Division of General Motors Corp. has been awarded two defense contracts totaling $57,500,000. One is a

Pontiac Motor Division was designated the "Design Agency" for this vehicle in 1951 subsequent to receiving assignment to build 203 carriers and do certain engine work in connection therewith. This designation required Engineering to make such changes in design as the Arsenal requested and our judgment dictated, and to carry out experimental and test work to insure [sic] satisfactory operation of the changed designs.

In addition to design and release work, the Engineering Department was authorized to build the first two pre-production vehicles in the Engineering shops. These two carriers were completed in February and put through 100[-] mile "break-in" tests at the General Motors Military Proving Ground. Rework of drawings to Ordnance requirements, with the exception of certain installation drawings, as well as the Ordnance Parts List, was completed April 14. During

A plywood mockup for the pilot T46, in a photo dated December 10, 1948, shows key elements that would carry over to the standardized vehicles: a sloping front deck, enclosed cab with two windshield panels and side entry doors, round windows in the cargo compartment, and wide tracks that ran on pneumatic tires. *Chun Hsu*

1952, a total of 1,576 releases and 6,306 changes were processed.

The Military services which will use this vehicle desired a number of design changes and, through the Arsenal, requested Pontiac Engineering, as the Design Agency, to submit proposals, drawings as well as cost and production data, on a total of thirty-nine major changes, eight of which were classified under a Revision "A" Program—being of top importance, and thirty-one of lesser importance were classified as Revision "B" changes. Last of the Revision "A" items, "Increased Capacity Bilge Pump" was released November 7 after extensive installations and capacity checks. Design and/ or disposition of all but five Revision "B" items was complete at the year end. Necessary cost information and production detail or technical reports were furnished the Arsenal regarding all items in the above Revision Programs.

In addition to a number of routine changes, miscellaneous T46E1 experimentation and/or design investigations included: transmission, rubber lip seals, auxiliary generator, four pinion final drive planetary set, heavy[-]duty innertubes, transmission lock-up speed, special maintenance tools, heater changes, weight specification revision, "On Vehicle Material" requirements, track manufacture investigation and durability and cab door latch. Experimental installation of combined track and marine steering, hydraulic propeller lift, litter carrier, and a surfing kit were slated for Ordnance observation on a vehicle assigned to the Engineering Department early in 1953.

The first full production vehicle was completed in May 1952 and was turned over to the Army the next month at a ceremony in Pontiac. Brig. Gen. C. H. Deitrick, commanding general of the Ordnance Tank Automotive Center, accepted the vehicle for the Army. Like all production vehicles, it had been completely assembled in Pontiac Plant 15, the company's pressed-metal plant, and but for the engine, the entire vehicle was manufactured by the Pontiac Motor Division.

A June 1952 Supplement to contract DA-20-018-ORD-12205 added an additional 196 vehicles to the contract, bringing the total to 399 contracted for at that time.

The 1953 Pontiac Engineering Annual Report sheds light on further development of the vehicle, stating:

In May, the vehicle name was changed from "Carrier, Cargo, Amphibious, T46E1" to "Carrier, Cargo, Amphibious, M76" and subsequent releases, change notices and references reflected said change.

As the "Design Agency" on the M76 (T46E1) Amphibious Cargo Carrier, Pontiac Product Engineering Department has processed a number of design changes. For this project, 521 releases and 4,157 change notices were issued during the year.

Revision "B" items—classified of lesser importance than Revision "A" items—released included a surfing kit and litter carrier.

Combined track and marine steering propeller lift, propeller guard, litter carrier, windshield wiper stops, surfing kit[,] and rear boarding handle installations were made on Engineering Vehicle #13 for inspection by Ordnance representatives. Functional approval of the above was received February 10.

Other miscellaneous M76 (T46E1) items receiving Engineering attention included: drive sprocket bearing lock,

A vehicle identified on the label of the original Detroit Arsenal photo as "Carrier, Amphibious, Cargo, T46," and dated May 5, 1950, is the first of two T46 pilots, registration no. 7041770. It featured the exhaust pipe and muffler on the left side of the vehicle and lacked the side fuel tanks that would be used on the pilot T46E1s and the production M76s. The trailing idler had been discarded in favor or a raised one. *Chun Hsu*

driver's escape hatch, for pinion final drive planetary set, track development, track adjustment maintenance tools, "On Vehicle Material" list release, side door latch, outer universal joint rubber boot, aluminum winch shear pin, spare parts, engine oil loss elimination, fuel injector failure investigations, auxiliary generator, and various drawing requirements.

Other M76 items released included several orthographic installation drawings to replace perspective type, a driver sprocket bearing lock, and work also was done on improvement of the present Winterization and Personnel Heater Kits.

In addition, the Engineering Department undertook the redesign of the Final Drive Planet Carrier in the transmission. Initiated by the General Motors Technical Center in 1952, the significant change concerned increasing the number of planet pinions from three to four in order to lengthen the service life of the unit. Tests run by the Ordnance Corps and by Pontiac indicated substantial improvement in this direction. However, cost of the initial design appeared to be too high. Because of the admitted desirability of this improvement, a new design was made by Pontiac which has very substantially lowered the cost and tooling charges. Drawings of the new design, along with a cost estimate, were submitted to the Ordnance Corps at the Detroit Arsenal.

The Otter-related narrative in the 1954 Pontiac Engineering Annual Report is considerably shorter than those of prior years but does contain some interesting information. The report states that the M76 and kits, less engine, contain 4,100 different parts, and in 1954 alone there were 942 engineering releases and changes notices related to the vehicle, which were documented on 64,500 square feet of drawings! The 1954 report goes on to state the following:

In addition, Pontiac Product Engineering built and supplied to the Detroit Arsenal eight sections of experimental track for testing at the Aberdeen Proving Ground; redrew track section assembly and details

This photo shows a T46 prototype from the rear, with the muffler and tailpipe mounted vertically on the rear of the left side of the hull. Two propellers are mounted between the tracks; the T46E1s and production M76s had one propeller. Pioneer tools and a door with hinges on the bottom were on the rear of the hull. *Chun Hsu*

to conform to General Motors Engineering Staff development, which are now being produced by the Pontiac Manufacturing Department under a spare[-]parts order; revised winterization kit and personnel heater installation, per Ordnance instructions; and designed, detailed[,] and processed release of a blackout lamp and horn guard. Three sets of exhaust manifolds and extensions were reworked by Engineering to replace Ryan couplings with flanges and gaskets for delivery to Detroit Arsenal for field installation as an experimental attempt to curtail carbon monoxide leaks. Six experimental oil cooler inlet tubes were fabricated and turned over to the Arsenal for subsequent Alaskan test.

On January 21, 1954, supplement number 9 to contract 12205 added a further 20 vehicles for the Marine Corps. This increased the total number of vehicles to be produced to 419. The supplement specified that these vehicles would be "equipped with additional modifications (Supp. No. 8) as required by the Marine Corps." Specifically these 20 machines (as well as the last 100 vehicles produced under the previous supplement, which were also destined for the Marine Corps) were to be equipped with: Litter Carrier kits Part no. 7977222; Combined Track & Marine Steering Kits, Part No. 7977201; Hydraulic Propeller Lift Kits, Part No. 7977200; and Surfing Kits, Part No. 7977241. The last of the final 20 Otters, and the last Otter period, was accepted and shipped on June 23, 1954.

The vehicle was used in areas with heavy snow, as well as extensively in Vietnam, where it was well suited to traversing rice paddies, marshes, swamps, lakes, and rivers. The Marines limited the operational area of the Otter in Vietnam because of the vulnerability of the vehicle's pneumatic tires as well as its lack of armor.

Top left: The Army contracted for three T46E1 pilot cargo carriers in June 1950, and these were completed and tested in 1951. A frontal photo of a pilot T46E1, registration no. 7041772, depicts the riveted aluminum-alloy skin, two service headlights, blackout marker lamps near the lower corners of the windshield, and a flexible spotlight on the cab roof. On the roof were two pan-shaped hatch doors for the driver and the codriver. On the left (driver's) side of the vehicle are a rearview mirror, a blackout driving light, and a horn. To the front of the windshield is the engine-access door, with a grab handle on the top and two cam locks to the front. *General Motors LLC*

On the rear of T46E1 no. 7041772 are two doors, with two leaf hinges on each one. To the left of the doors are pioneer tools. Below the doors is a tow pintle, below which is the mounting for a propeller. *General Motors LLC*

On the left side of T46E1 no. 7041773 was an external fuel tank, a round window with a metal-screen guard inside, and a spare bogie wheel. The driver's door had two front hinges, a rubber seal around its inner perimeter, and a rain gutter above it. The sprockets were rubber covered. The bogie wheels, mounted in pairs on torsion bars, were equipped with size 6.60 × 15 pneumatic no-tread, ten-ply tires. *General Motors LLC*

On the right side of the same vehicle were two 5-gallon liquid containers, a round window in the cargo compartment, a ladder for accessing the roof (not present on production M76 Otters), a fuel tank, and the codriver's door. The pilot T46E1s had smaller fuel tanks than the ones on production M76s, with their bottoms being slightly above the bottoms of the side doors. *General Motors LLC*

Pilot T46E1, registration no. 7041773, was the subject of winter testing at Devil's Lake, North Dakota, in February 1951. The light-colored object on the ladder is a placard. Stored on the edge of the roof of the cargo compartment is a boat hook. *Ordnance Museum*

In a left view of no. 7041773 at Devil's Lake in February 1951, the propeller is installed on its mount. The propeller was designed to tilt upward when the boat was operating on land. It was powered by a driveshaft from a power takeoff. The T46E1 proved very capable in deep snow and had the ability to proceed through snow up to 30 inches in depth. *Ordnance Museum*

The T46E1 was approved for production and standardized as the M76 amphibious cargo carrier. The first production Otter is accepted by Brig. Gen. C. H. Deitrick, commanding general of the Ordnance Tank Automotive Center (*second from left*). At left is Arnold Lenz, Pontiac general manager. To the general's left are Col. Paul Seleen, deputy district chief, Detroit Ordnance District; A. F. Johnson, manufacturing manager; and Buel Starr, Pontiac general manufacturing manager. *General Motors LLC*

As seen in this photo of an M76 undergoing testing, the fuel tanks were taller than those of the pilot and had a capacity of 35 gallons. In addition, two stiffeners were added to the outer sides of the bottom of the bow, in addition to the two stiffeners that were present on the T46E1s. *General Motors LLC*

The pan-shaped top hatch doors are visible on the cab roof. A flexible spotlight is mounted between them. Aft of the hatches on the roof are the engine exhaust tailpipe and two cargo-hatch doors. On top of the right fuel tank is the filler cap. *General Motors LLC*

An M76 is proceeding up a ramp during testing. The Otter could negotiate a 60 percent grade, or a slope of 31 degrees. The positions and shapes of the stiffeners on the bottom of the bow are visible. *General Motors LLC*

The M76 is observed from the right side while performing a climbing test. The pioneer tools had been relocated to the rear of the side of the hull. The purpose of the trapezoidal object below the round window, which was a standard accessory for the M76, has been enigmatic, but on the basis of a study of diagrams of the M76, its shape and size match the opening on the roof for the engine exhaust, so it is possible that it was a hood for that opening. *General Motors LLC*

An image of the M76 nearing the top of the ramp shows some features on the roof: the drivers' hatches; the engine exhaust, surrounded by louvers on top of a fairing; and the cargo doors. On the rear of the vehicle are two doors, two taillight assemblies, steps, a tow pintle, and the propeller, folded upward for travel. *General Motors LLC*

The M76 performed well on mucky ground as well as in water. This example is about to enter a body of water during testing. The propeller has been folded down for use. On the upper corners of the rear of the hull are lifting eyes, on reinforced plates that wrap around the corners. *General Motors LLC*

The M76 is chugging along on a lake during a test run. The curved tailpipe is above the roof between the drivers' hatches. A single grab handle is near the left-rear corner of the roof. Rivets are present on the hull in profusion; the aluminum-alloy skin was riveted to a steel frame. Steel plates on the inside of the hull were used to anchor features such as steps, spare tires, and fuel tanks. The headlights were mounted on round plates that were screwed to the deck.

The same M76 is exiting from the lake. Whereas the smaller fuel tanks of the T46E1 had two separate bands around them, for attaching the tanks to the hull, the taller tanks of the M46 lacked the bands but had three thin, horizontal ribs around them. *General Motors LLC*

Powering the M76 Otter was a Continental AO-268-3A 268-cubic-inch, 135-horsepower, air-cooled, fuel-injected engine (*top*), directly coupled to a Pontiac cross-drive automatic transmission (*bottom*). The view is from the left rear, showing the fan on the rear of the engine. *General Motors LLC*

As seen in a view of the M76 emerging from the lake, each of the tracks of the M76 Otter was constructed of three flexible belts, two narrow outer ones and one wide central one, to which metal track shoes were riveted. Each tier of track shoes consisted of two sections, with one being riveted to the inner belt and the center belt, and the other one being riveted to the outer belt and the center belt. *General Motors LLC*

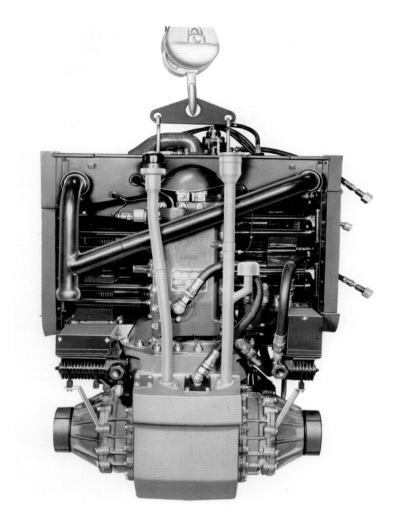

The power pack, consisting of the AO-268-3A engine over the Pontiac cross-drive transmission, is viewed from the right rear. At the top are a lifting hook and sling. *General Motors LLC*

The power pack for the M76 is observed from the front. The engine was a four-cylinder, horizontal-opposed design. *General Motors LLC*

Two US Army officers and a civilian are standing alongside a power pack on a stand, next to an M76. Hanging to the left of the engine are the controls for the hoist. *General Motors LLC*

Technicians are assembling Pontiac cross-drive transmissions for installation in M76s. The nearest transmission is seen from the right rear, with the right final drive yet to be mounted on the side. *General Motors LLC*

A Continental AO-268-3A engine is seen in the front of an M76, with the access hatch secured open. Visible in the opening in the aft bulkhead of the engine compartment is the top of the fan shroud. *General Motors LLC*

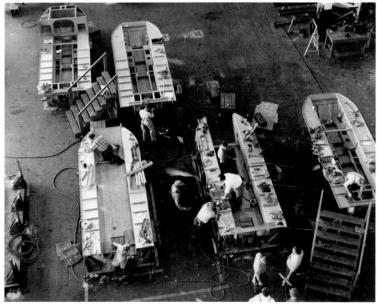

The Pontiac Division of General Motors built pilot T46E1s and the production M76s, completing the first M76 in May 1952 and completing the last of four hundred M76s in June 1954. Here, seven hulls under construction are visible in an overhead view. The hull toward the upper left has advanced to the point where the floor framing and the engine-compartment bulkheads have been installed. *General Motors LLC*

Upper hulls are under construction at the Pontiac plant. Visible through the assistant driver's door of the M76 in the foreground is part of the bulkhead between the cab and the cargo compartment. On the next chassis on the line, the bow is under construction. *General Motors LLC*

Workers are cleaning an M76 hull before it enters the paint booth, *right*, for an overall coat of paint. Visible through the stern door and the round window are dark-colored vertical frame members in the cargo compartment. Faintly visible here as well as in the closest hull in the preceding photo are five vertical stiffeners in the area where the right fuel tank will be mounted. *General Motors LLC*

M76s in various states of completion are on the Pontiac Division factory floor. The nearest vehicles have their cargo-hatch doors, driver's hatch doors, and engine-compartment doors installed. These doors haven't been installed yet on vehicles farther to the rear. *General Motors LLC*

Painters are spraying a coat on an M76 hull. Masking material has been applied over the windshields, the engine-compartment hatch, and headlights, and drop cloths have been draped over the tracks to protect them from overspray. *General Motors LLC*

"Rosie the Riveter" was a nickname given to American women who worked in the manufacturing sector in World War II. Although the photo was taken six or seven years after the end of the war, these two women very much fit in the mold, in that they are assembling tracks for M76s by riveting track shoes to the flexible bands that are laid out on the bench to the front of them. Assembled sections of tracks are in the foreground. *General Motors LLC*

Nicknamed "Swamp Otter," this restored M76 Otter is in the collection of John Cheney II. It is an early-type vehicle, with the fuel tanks mounted to the immediate rear of the cab doors. *Tracy White*

A slightly elevated view of "Swamp Otter" shows some details on the upper deck, including the driver's and assistant driver's pan-shaped hatch doors, the spotlight, the fairing between those doors and the enclosed engine-exhaust pipe, and the open cargo-hatch doors. *Tracy White*

The respective locations of features on the right side are illustrated. Stored pioneer tools include a shovel, ax, and mattock head. The trapezoidal "mystery" fixture, thought to be a cover for the opening for the exhaust on the top deck, is stored below the round window. *Tracy White*

An elevated frontal view shows the engine-compartment cover, the service headlights, the blackout marker lamps to the fronts of the lower corners of the windshield, grab handles near the sides of the front deck, and a closed chock on the front of the deck. *Tracy White*

The tracks with the narrow, outer bands and the wide central bands, connected by riveted-on track shoes, are seen to good advantage, as are the four vertical stiffeners on the lower part of the bow. The 30-inch-wide tracks gave the Otter plenty of flotation on snow and soft terrain. Tow eyes and clevises are on the undersides of the fronts of the sponsons. *Tracy White*

The pneumatic rubber tires of the bogie wheels are seated in the guide portions of the track shoes. Each bogie-wheel assembly includes two wheels and two tires. *Tracy White*

The curved engine-exhaust pipe is visible above the upper deck of the Otter. In the shadows above the spare bogie wheel is a 5-gallon liquid container. *Tracy White*

"Swamp Otter" is observed from the upper front left. On the bottom front of the driver's door is a scissors-type doorstop. A cam lock with a handle is to the front of the driver's hatch as well as the assistant driver's. A screen is over the open side of the fairing around the engine-exhaust pipe. *Tracy White*

The rear doors of the cargo compartment are open, revealing several of the vertical frame members on the right wall of that compartment. Also in view is the three-bladed propeller, lowered into its position for operating in water. *Tracy White*

From August 1952 until the end of production in June 1954, the two fuel tanks were relocated to the rears of the sides of the hull. This revision necessitated moving accessories to new locations. A step and grab handle, for accessing the upper deck, were now mounted to the rear of the driver's door. Between the step and the fuel tank, a 5-gallon liquid container, a spare bogie wheel and tire, and an ax were stored. *General Motors LLC*

The propeller of this post-August 1952 Otter is equipped with a guard. To the front of the fuel tank is a shovel, and to the rear of the driver's door are a mattock handle and head. *General Motors LLC*

An overhead view of a post-August 1952 Otter shows the positions and shapes of the driver's and the assistant driver's hatch doors, the trapezoidal fairing between the hatches, and the cargo-hatch doors. The driver's hatch had a hinge on the rear, while the assistant driver's hatch lacked a hinge; instead it swiveled when opened and closed. *General Motors LLC*

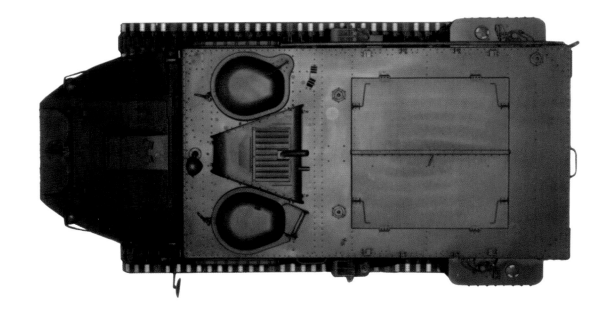

M76 Otter, registration no. 7041856, exhibits the rear fuel tanks of a vehicle completed after August 1952. On the bow are markings for the Test Operation of Army Field Forces Board No. 2. *Kevin Emdee collection*

The right side of the same M76 is viewed broadside. In addition to necessitating the relocation of the pioneer tools, the new positions of the fuel tanks mandated that the round windows of the cargo compartment be moved forward. *Kevin Emdee collection*

US Army M76, registration no. 13A397, is the subject of a photo dated November 12, 1958. The 5-gallon liquid container rests on an angle iron attached to the hull, and is secured in place with a strap. Two grab handles are near the forward corners of the engine-compartment cover; the left handle is partially hidden by the left service headlight. *TACOM LCMC History Office*

A photo dated January 30, 1960, shows US Army M76, registration no. 13A470, from the left front. Marked on the upper right corner of the bow is "APG-D&PS," which stands for Aberdeen Proving Ground, Development and Proof Services. *TACOM LCMC History Office*

The driver's hatch door is open on this early-type M76 with fuel tanks to the immediate rears of the cab doors. "PROPELLER" is painted on the side of the bow, to remind personnel around the vehicle that an operable propeller is present. Stenciled on the front of the bow is "M76" over "NO.25." The Army registration number on the door is difficult to discern but appears to be 7041732. The photo bears the date May 8, 1961. *TACOM LCMC History Office*

This M76, with registration no. 13A470, has the rear-mounted fuel tanks, in a photo dated October 10, 1961. Although the pneumatic tires on the bogie wheels had no treads, dust and mud left an imprint on them, through gaps in the tracks, sometimes giving the tires the appearance of having treads. *TACOM LCMC History Office*

An M76 Otter from the 3rd Marine Division is crossing a river during Operation Prairie, a US offensive in Quang Tri Province, Republic of Vietnam, from early August 1966 to January 31, 1967. Above the assistant driver's hatch is a ring mount for a machine gun: the cradle and ammunition-box holder are visible, but a machine gun is not mounted. The Marine seated above that hatch is holding an M14 rifle. *National Archives and Records Administration*

A heavily mud-spattered M76, registration no. 348043, from the 3rd Marine Division pauses in front of a command post during Operation Prairie, sometime between August 1966 and January 1967. A clear view is available of the ring mount above the assistant driver's hatch, with an M2 HB .50-caliber machine gun installed on it. *National Archives and Records Administration*

During a resupply mission to the 9th Marines during Operation Chinook II on February 22, 1967, an M76 Otter from Headquarters and Service Company, 3rd Motor Transport Battalion, 3rd Marines, is negotiating a rice-paddy dike. Three Marines are standing up in the cargo hatch, and another one is manning a .50-caliber machine gun on a ring mount, or skate rail. The head of yet another Marine is above the driver's hatch. Below the round window on the side of the cargo compartment is the pan-shaped carrier for the spare bogie wheel. *National Archives and Records Administration*

Members of III Marine Amphibious Force (MAF) are about to begin a patrol mission in an Otter, registration no. 176725, at Khe Sanh during Operation Scotland on January 29, 1968. An ammunition chest is on the cab roof. Stenciled on the side of the driver's door are "ENTRY HATCH" over "DO NOT SLAM DOOR" over a black-spade symbol. A black-spade symbol is also on the bow, and the name "LINDA" is very faintly visible below the registration number. *National Archives and Records Administration*

The M76 Otter proved adept at transiting the rice paddies that were prevalent in Vietnam. This example, Marine Corps registration no. 221873, is ferrying Marines across a paddy during Operation Saline, on April 26, 1968. The ring-mounted .50-caliber machine gun gave the vehicle a potent defensive and offensive punch. An armor plate was mounted to the front of the windshield; a visor is faintly visible on the plate to the front of the driver's position. *National Archives and Records Administration*

Members of Hotel Company, 2nd Battalion, 4th Marines, are unloading C rations and other supplies from an Otter for Vietnamese civilians during a medcap mission north of Cua Viet on April 25, 1968. Medcaps were medical and economic aid missions in support of the Vietnamese populace. The rail of a ring mount is visible to the upper right. *National Archives and Records Administration*

The previously depicted M76 with registration no. 221873 is on the advance during a firefight during Operation Napoleon/Saline, near Dai Do, east of Dong Ha, in May 1968. The vehicle was from 2nd Battalion, 4th Marines. This vehicle had an enclosure around the ring mount, evidently to provide extra protection to the gunner, and an armor plate with a visor on the front of the windshield. *National Archives and Records Administration*

An M76, registration no. 176706, is emerging from a river and entering an outpost, Camp Big John, west of Cua Viet, Republic of Vietnam, on July 29, 1968. The right fuel tank has been noticeably battered. The Marine to the left is hanging on to the .50-caliber machine gun mount; the gun has been dismounted. *National Archives and Records Administration*

USMC 176706

Certain components of the Otter required daily maintenance. Cpl. A. M. Carvella is lubricating the suspension of a 1st Marine Regiment M76, registration no. 221892, at Camp Big John on June 29, 1968. The vehicle is resting on a platform, presumably to allow access for maintenance to the bottom of the hull and inner sides of the suspension. *National Archives and Records Administration*

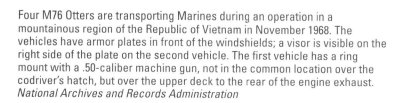

Four M76 Otters are transporting Marines during an operation in a mountainous region of the Republic of Vietnam in November 1968. The vehicles have armor plates in front of the windshields; a visor is visible on the right side of the plate on the second vehicle. The first vehicle has a ring mount with a .50-caliber machine gun, not in the common location over the codriver's hatch, but over the upper deck to the rear of the engine exhaust. *National Archives and Records Administration*

A column of M76s from the 3rd Marine Division are crossing a stream on a mission to a Montagnard village on November 22, 1968. The hulls are mostly brown, from exposure to dust and mud. *National Archives and Records Administration*

A Marine is sprawled out on the forward deck of an M76 Otter from III Marine Amphibious Force during Operation Meade River, southeast of Da Nang, on December 4, 1968. Otters, including this one, as well as helicopters had been engaged in resupplying Marine units in that area, as part of the operation. The Marine in the assistant driver's hatch is carrying a movie camera. *National Archives and Records Administration*

As seen from the upper deck of an M76 Otter, another Otter is navigating a stream south of Cau Lu in Vietnam on January 28, 1969. In the right foreground, the .50-caliber machine gun is trained aft. Below it is a curved piece of armor. The machine gun doesn't seem to be mounted on the ring mount of the Otter to the rear. Armor plate is on the windshield of that vehicle. *National Archives and Records Administration*

This M76, registration no. 176691, with rear-mounted fuel tanks and a ring mount, was one of five Otters that were rebuilt by the Motor Transport Maintenance Company of the US Marine Corps' Force Logistics Command, Vietnam, in 1969. The ring mount on an adjacent M76 is to the right. *National Archives and Records Administration*

General Data	
Model	M76
Weight*	12,162
Max. towed load	6,000 lbs.
Length**	188
Width**	98
Height**	108
Std. track width	30
Max. speed, land/water	28 mph / 4.5 mph
Fuel capacity	70 gal.
Range, land	160 miles
Electrical	24 negative
Transmission speeds	2
Turning-radius feet	pivot

Engine Data	
Engine make/model	Continental AOI-268-3A
Number of cylinders	4 opposed
Cubic-inch displacement	269
Horsepower	127 @ 3,200
Torque	225 @ 2,600
Governed speed, rpm	3,200

* Fighting weight, in pounds
** Overall dimensions listed in inches

CHAPTER 2
The M116/XM733 Husky

Designed as the replacement for the M29 Weasel tracked carrier of World War II vintage, the T116 Husky amphibious cargo carrier was a fully tracked, lightweight design. Development of the vehicle commenced in November 1956. A still from a movie documenting the preliminary operation of the T116 amphibious cargo carrier shows one of the three pilot vehicles speeding along a test course. This example lacked the upper hull and cab enclosure. On each side were five spoked dual bogie wheels, with drive sprockets to the front and idler guide wheels to the rear. The driver was seated on the left side. *PACCAR, Inc.*

In 1950, the Army Equipment Development Guide set out the requirements for amphibious cargo carriers in three weight classes (½ ton, 1½ ton, and 2½ ton) and further specified that the ground pressure for each of these was not to exceed 2 pounds per square inch. The T46E1, for which production contracts were just being issued, met the criteria for the 1½-ton-capacity vehicle, albeit slightly exceeding the specified ground pressure. To meet the ½-ton requirement, Studebaker was developing the T107 as a replacement for its highly successful M29C Weasel.

However, the T107 did not prove to be a successful design and thus did not enter production. In November 1956, a new development program for an amphibious cargo carrier was launched, with attention once again focusing on a 1½-ton-capacity vehicle, designated the T116. On May 3, 1957, a development contract was issued to American Car and Foundry Company of Renton, Washington, to design and construct four pilot examples of the T116. Pacific shipped the first example to Aberdeen for testing on November 27, 1958. Not quite a month later, December 22, a second pilot was shipped, this one to the Arctic Test Board.

Testing of these vehicles indicated deficiencies in the air-cooled Continental 8AO-198 opposed-cylinder engines as well as the Hydramatic 198-M transmission.

Accordingly, the Army directed that these components be replaced with a liquid-cooled Chevrolet 283 V-8 and military standard 301 Hydramatic transmission. Once repowered, the designation of the vehicles were changed to T116E1.

Subsequent to further testing, the modified vehicles were classified as Standard A on December 15, 1960, and at the same time the payload rating of the vehicle was raised from ½ ton to 1½ ton. It was christened the Husky, and Pacific Car and Foundry was awarded a contract to manufacture three preproduction pilots. However, the actual production contract, awarded December 15, 1961, went to Blaw-Knox Company. The firm's construction equipment division, located in Mattoon, Illinois, would produce the vehicles under a $4.5 million contract. The company would build 197 of the vehicles, with Construction Equipment Division manager Robert Thornburg telling the *Mattoon Daily Journal-Gazette*, "We expect to begin production of the carrier and related items in July 1962 and compete the contract by February 1963."

As it turned out, the company publication *B-K News*, in October 1962, reported that "the first units produced at the plant were run off the assembly line during the first week of October 1962."

The *Daily Journal-Gazette*, on Tuesday, October 30, 1963, reported, "The first of 200 one and one-half ton M116 amphibious cargo carriers to be turned off the assembly line at the Blaw-Knox Company plant here passed an important phase of its government acceptance tests at Lake Mattoon Monday afternoon."

On May 18, 1963, the company announced that it had received a contract extension for the production of additional M116 vehicles.

The aluminum-bodied, welded-construction, 6,700-pound vehicle had a capacity of ten men in winter gear or twelve men in summer gear in addition to the driver.

In 1962, the Tank Automotive Center adapted an M116 chassis to form the basis of a two-man lightweight armored assault vehicle, which was tested at Aberdeen Proving Ground in July 1965. The vehicle was equipped with a two-gun cupola and a third gun mounted in the center of the hull front. This vehicle was ultimately designated the XM729.

In February 1965, the Army began developing a second armored variant of the M116. This vehicle, designated the XM733, had an open top and was armed with 7.62 mm and .50-caliber machine guns. A variant of the XM733, the XM733E1, featured a cupola to protect the gunner.

In October 1966, the Army lost interest in the XM733 and canceled the program. However, the Marine Corps had considerable interest and by 1967 had awarded a ninety-three-vehicle production contract to the Pacific Car and Foundry Company.

This was followed by another contract, awarded by the Corps on December 22, 1966, for 111 unarmored XM733s. An "unarmored XM733" is essentially an M116, and thus these vehicles were designated M116A1, the first of which were delivered in December 1967.

The T116 Husky featured a welded aluminum-alloy hull with a low silhouette. The vehicle boasted a low ground pressure, less than 2.5 psi at 10,000 pounds of gross vehicle weight, resulting in excellent mobility on snow and soft ground. This photo, dated September 16, 1958, depicts one of three preproduction pilot T116s manufactured by Pacific Car and Foundry. It featured an enclosed cab; a winch between the headlights; a fabric "summer" closure, or cover, with soft plastic windows for the cargo compartment; and side skirts, known as track shrouds. *TACOM LCMC History Office*

A winter closure kit was developed for the T116, comprising a hard top with three windows on each side and two on the rear. The rear windows were on a panel equipped with a piano hinge on the top; below that panel was a tailgate with three leaf hinges on the bottom and a lock handle on the upper center. On the right side of the cab was the air-exhaust grille, through which engine-cooling air and engine exhaust exited the vehicle. The T116s were powered by the Continental 8A0-198 air-cooled engine through a Hydramatic 198-M transmission. *TACOM LCMC History Office*

Pilot T116, registration no. 13A883, was delivered to Aberdeen Proving Ground for testing in late November 1958. In this photo, dated January 14, 1959, a soldier poses next to the vehicle, for scale, during testing at Aberdeen. The vehicle was painted overall in Olive Drab (the windshield gaskets are a darker tone of OD), but the frame of the driver's side window is bare metal. On the bow is a winch, flanked by the recessed headlight assemblies. The bottom of the front of the hull had a ribbed design, as seen on the bow. *US Army Ordnance TSF*

Pilot T116, registration no. 13A883, is viewed from the left side during tests at Aberdeen Proving Ground on January 14, 1959. Below the second side window was a vent, which did not become a standard feature on the production M116s. The track apron was hinged and is secured in its raised position. *US Army Ordnance TSF*

A rear view of pilot T116, registration no. 13A883, during tests at Aberdeen in January 1959 shows the two windows on the rear of the closure, as well as the tailgate, with three leaf hinges on its bottom. This closure is the summer version of canvas construction. Taillight assemblies are on the upper corners of the rear of the hull, with a lifting eye on the inboard side of each taillight. Stencils indicating the locations of pioneer tools are on the rear of the hull. *US Army Ordnance TSF*

The pilot T116 tested at Aberdeen in late 1958 and early 1959 is observed from above with the cab top and the cargo-compartment closure removed. In the cab were two single seats, with an upholstered bench seat between them. Aft of the seats is the engine compartment, and to the rear is the cargo compartment. *US Army Ordnance TSF*

The same pilot T116 is viewed from the left, with the cab and cargo-compartment closures removed and the track apron secured in the raised position. A boat hook is secured to brackets on the side of the upper hull. *US Army Ordnance TSF*

Owing to problems with the T116's Continental engine during testing, four pilot vehicles, built by Pacific Car and Foundry, were fitted with Chevrolet V-8, 283-cubic-inch, water-cooled engines and military-standard Hydramatic transmissions and were designated T116E1s. Testing indicated that these vehicles were satisfactory, and the model was standardized as the "Amphibious Cargo Carrier M116" in December 1960. In a photo dated February 9, 1961, this pilot T116E1, registration no. 13A885, is equipped with a winter closure kit. On the center rear of the cab top deck is the engine-air intake grille. On the winter closure roof were two doors. *TACOM LCMC History Office*

During evaluation, this T116E1, registration no. 13A883, carried Aberdeen Proving Ground markings on the bow. A recess was built into each side of the hull above the front bogie wheel for a step. Below the front side window of the cab is the latch for the driver's hatch door. The original front lifting rings (outboard of the headlights) had a distinctly light-duty appearance. *TACOM LCMC History Office*

In mid-May 1959, pilot T116E1, registration no. 13A883, is undergoing a water test on the Conowingo Reservoir on the Susquehanna River in Maryland, a short distance north of Aberdeen Proving Ground. The cab doors are open, and the canvas cargo-compartment closure seen in the preceding photos has been replaced by a winter enclosure, of rigid construction, with large, dual hatch doors on the roof. *US Army Ordnance TSF*

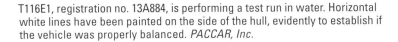

T116E1, registration no. 13A884, is performing a test run in water. Horizontal white lines have been painted on the side of the hull, evidently to establish if the vehicle was properly balanced. *PACCAR, Inc.*

The same T116E1 is shown after a water test. The horizontal white lines on the side of the hull are visible. At the upper left corner of the rear of the hull is the left taillight assembly, containing the left stoplight-taillight over a blackout marker light. The right taillight assembly had a blackout stoplight over the right stoplight-taillight. Below the tailgate is the tow pintle. *PACCAR, Inc.*

This series of color photographs was taken during desert testing of T116E1, registration no. 13A886. Tape has been applied over the winch on the center of the bow. This winch had a capacity of up to 6,000 pounds. The winter closure is installed, rather than the seemingly more appropriate summer closure. Although difficult to discern, the front lifting eyes on this vehicle were reinforced and were similar or identical to those on production M116s. *Kevin Emdee collection*

A right-side view of the T116E1 includes the air-exhaust grille, above the "T-116E1" inscription on the hull. A series of leaf springs on the top of the track shrouds permitted the shrouds to be raised for maintenance and repair of the suspension and the tracks. *Kevin Emdee collection*

The same T116E1 is viewed from the right rear during desert testing. A 5-gallon liquid container is stored on a holder to each side of the tailgate. Above each container, and outboard of the taillight assembly, is a lifting eye. Below the tailgate are pioneer tools: an ax, shovel, mattock handle, and mattock head. *Kevin Emdee collection*

Pilot T116E1, registration no. 13A886, is entering the water, bow first. A flexible engine-exhaust hose is jutting out of the opening in the lower-rear corner of the air-exhaust grille. The driver's and passenger's hatch doors are folded, one over the other, on the cab roof. *Kevin Emdee collection*

The same T116E1 pilot is crossing a body of water during testing. The tracks provided propulsion during operations in water. The water pouring out of the opening on the side of the bow is from the bilge pump. *Kevin Emdee collection*

US Army military policemen are manning pilot T116E1, registration no. 13A885, during winter testing. The track shroud on this vehicle is the Hydrovane version, which would become standard on production M116s, on both sides of the vehicle. The Hydrovane shrouds improved the vehicle's performance in water and had vertical louvers on the front half; the rear half resembled that part of the original track shrouds. *Chun Hsu*

The T116E1 was standardized as the "Amphibious Cargo Carrier M116" in mid-December 1961. Pacific Car and Foundry built three preproduction M116s, including this example, registration no. 6E2671. The reinforced front lifting rings are in view. A spare-track section is stored on the bow. Four small eyebolts, two on the cab roof and two to the sides of the roof doors of the winter closure, are a new addition. *TACOM LCMC History Office*

In a photo dated November 9, 1961, preproduction M116 6E2671 exhibits non-Hydrovane track shrouds without the cutouts below the steps on the sides of the hull. A "LIFT HERE" stencil is on the base of the left front lifting eye. In a recess below the rear side window of the cab is the fuel filler cap. *TACOM LCMC History Office*

In another photo dated November 9, 1961, Hydrovane track shrouds have been installed. The small, round object on the center of the tailgate was a doorstop. *TACOM LCMC History Office*

A front view of the same preproduction M116 shows the recessed headlight assemblies and winch, the spare-track section, and the ribs on the bottom of the bow. *TACOM LCMC History Office*

In a photo dated November 9, 1961, the same preproduction M116 is fitted with non-Hydrovane track shrouds; the right one has been raised and secured in the open position. Obviously, having the shrouds raised would make it difficult for the driver and passenger to enter the cab, since the shrouds would cover the steps in the hull. *TACOM LCMC History Office*

Preproduction M116, registration no. 6E2671, is viewed from the upper left rear, with doors and tailgate open. A strut on each side supports the raised rear door of the winter closure. Seat cushions are installed in the cargo compartment. The vehicle could carry eleven troops with winter gear, or thirteen with summer gear. *Chun Hsu*

As seen in a view of 6E2671 dated November 9, 1961, with the cab cover and the winter closure removed, the cargo compartment had an adjustable floor, which could be raised to form a continuous flatbed compartment. Features of the engine-compartment cover in the rear of the cab are in view. *Chun Hsu*

Another of the three Pacific Car and Foundry–built preproduction M116s was registration number 6E2672, seen here in a factory or shop without a closure over the cargo compartment. Hydrovane track shrouds are installed.

General Data	
Model	**M116**
Weight*	10,600
Length**	188.1
Width**	82.1
Height**	79.1
Max. speed, land/water	37 mph / 4.2 mph
Fuel capacity	65 gal.
Range, land	300 miles
Electrical	24 negative
Transmission speeds	4F, 1R
Turning radius, feet	8

* Fighting weight, in pounds
** Overall dimensions listed in inches

Engine Data	
Engine make/model	**Chevrolet**
Number of cylinders	V-8
Cubic-inch displacement	283
Horsepower	160 @ 4,600
Torque	210 @ 2,400
Governed speed, rpm	4,600

Preproduction M116 6E2672 is viewed from the right rear with the cab enclosure installed. On the rear of that enclosure are two windows, between which, in a recess, is a dome light. The small, square feature to the immediate rear of the "US ARMY" marking is a fuel vent; an identical one was on the opposite side of the hull. Below them were stencils that read "CAUTION FUEL VENT."

In a right side view of 6E2672, the positions of the rear lifting rings are evident. The engine-air exhaust grille was fitted with a piano hinge on the bottom of the frame, and two latch knobs on the top of the frame. A round hole is present on each guide horn of the tracks.

Preproduction M116, registration no. 6E2673, is equipped with Hydrovane track shrouds in this photo dated February 14, 1962. The spare-track section is not mounted on the bow, allowing a view of the four brackets for attaching the track section. *TACOM LCMC History Office*

The same preproduction M116 is observed from the rear, with two 5-gallon liquid containers strapped to the hull and pioneer tools in their assigned positions below the tailgate. A 12-inch ruler is standing to the rear of the right track. *Chun Hsu*

This final view of a preproduction M116 was taken at Aberdeen Proving Ground on November 9, 1961, and shows the vehicle from above the front end. The positions of the cab doors, the engine-air intake grille, and the winter-closure top doors are evident. Each cab door consists of a top panel and a side panel with a window; each door has a piano hinge attaching the top panel to the cab roof, and another piano hinge joining the top and the side panels. *Chun Hsu*

Blaw-Knox Company, manufacturers of road-construction equipment in Mattoon, Illinois, carried out series production of the M116s. The Army issued the contract on December 15, 1961, and production commenced in mid-1962. Originally, two hundred M116s were completed under the contract, but in May 1962, Blaw-Knox received an add-on contract totaling $1 million to produce additional M116s. Seen here is the first production M116 built by Blaw-Knox, registration no. 13B007, about to enter the water during a manufacturer's test. *Chun Hsu*

The second production M116, registration no. 13B008, is being test-driven up a muddy embankment. No cab or cargo-compartment enclosures are installed. At the center of the hull is a vertical line, running through the "S" in "US ARMY," marked "CG" (center of gravity) at the bottom. *TACOM LCMC History Office*

M116 13B008 is negotiating a muddy flat during manufacturer's testing. Faintly visible in the cargo compartment are the tops of a number of 5-gallon liquid containers. *TACOM LCMC History Office*

A summer closure made of fabric, with soft-plastic windows, is fitted over the cargo compartment of this M116, registration no. 13B022. Two radio antennas are mounted on the rear corners of the cab roof. "TEST OPERATION" is painted in white on the side of the cab. *TACOM LCMC History Office*

B-K-NEWS

VOLUME 16, NO. 10   PITTSBURGH, PA.   OCTOBER, 1962

At our Construction Equipment Division—

Blaw-Knox Employees Build Light-Weight, Rugged and

Mobile Amphibious Cargo Carrier for U. S. Army

The Blaw-Knox Company's in-house publication, *B-K News*, featured an article on the M116 in its October 1962 issue. This cover photo shows workers in the Construction Equipment Division performing assembly operations on the Chevrolet V-8 engine and the cargo compartment.

Shop foremen are inspecting welds on the upper hull of an M116. With the tailgate not yet installed, the interior of the cargo compartment, including its forward bulkhead, is visible. Pentagonal frames on the upper corners of the rear of the upper hull are for attaching the rear lifting eyes and the taillight assemblies.

A Blaw-Knox worker is preparing one of several Chevrolet V-8 engines for installation in M116s. Attached to the rear of the engine is the transmission: a military-standard Hydramatic.

This M116, registration no. 13B285, was restored by and is owned by Ron Fitzpatrick. Bows are installed over the cargo compartment for supporting a summer closure. A small, round rearview mirror replaces the larger, rectangular ones on the left side of the windshield. *Ron Fitzpatrick*

A rear view of the same M116 shows the stored positions of the ax, shovel, and mattock head and handle, along with the corresponding retainer straps and brackets. "LIFT HERE" labels, white with black lettering, are on the rear lifting rings. *Ron Fitzpatrick*

On the basis of the favorable performance of the M116, the US Army decided to experiment with an assault vehicle based on the M116 chassis in the early 1960s. This plywood mockup featured a glacis with a curved top and a centrally located bow machine gun in a ball mount. The driver's station had vision blocks on the front and sides and a top hatch door with a periscope. A cupola also incorporated vision blocks and had mounts for two .30-caliber machine guns. On the rear deck are engine-air grilles and an engine exhaust.

In the mid-1960s, the Tank Automotive Center modified an existing experimental vehicle based on the M116, designated the Aluminum Armor Test Rig, resulting in the Armored Assault Vehicle Test Rig, as seen during testing at Aberdeen Proving Ground on or before August 3, 1965. The Armored Assault Vehicle Test Rig featured a fixed structure between the headlights, which may have functioned as a surfboard. The dome-shaped, manually powered cupola, with all-around vision blocks, was armed with two machine guns. *US Army Ordnance TSF*

In February 1965, the Army began development of an armored assault vehicle based on the M116 chassis, designated the XM733. It was an open-topped carrier, capable of mounting several combinations of weapons. In this photo, taken at Aberdeen Proving Ground and dated November 23, 1965, the vehicle, serial no. 13B084, is armed with an M175 40 mm automatic grenade launcher with a flexible ammunition chute in the forward station. A Browning M1919 .30-caliber machine gun and an M60 7.62 mm machine gun are visible above the fighting compartment. *US Army Ordnance TSF*

The layout of the driver's station, the forward weapon station, and the fighting compartment of the XM733 is viewed from above in a photo dated November 10, 1965. The weapons are configured as in the preceding photo. The engine compartment is between the forward weapon station and the fighting compartment. *US Army Ordnance TSF*

The XM733 is viewed from the front, showing how the forward weapon station and its shield are offset slightly to the right of the center of the vehicle. Mounted on that station is an M175 40 mm automatic grenade launcher. *US Army Ordnance TSF*

An XM733, registration no. 13B084, is viewed from the rear, armed with an M175 40 mm grenade launcher, two .30-caliber machine guns, and two M60 7.62 mm machine guns. *US Army Ordnance TSF*

In the configuration shown in this left-front view of XM733 registration no. 13B084, an M60 7.62 mm machine gun is mounted in the forward station, and another one is in the left rear of the fighting compartment. The forward station was slightly to the right of the front-to-rear centerline and was equipped with a shield on the front and sides. *Rock Island Arsenal Museum*

At Aberdeen on November 10, 1965, the XM733 is configured with an M175 40 mm automatic grenade launcher in the forward station, a Browning M1919 .30-caliber air-cooled machine gun in each front corner of the fighting compartment, and an M60 machine gun in each rear corner of the fighting compartment. A tailgate with three hinges on the bottom is on the rear of the fighting compartment. *US Army Ordnance TSF*

The XM733E1 with the cupola for the 40 mm grenade launcher is observed from the right side, with the turret and grenade launcher oriented to the front. *US Army Ordnance TSF*

In a left-rear view of the XM733E1, the lower part of the cupola is in view; it had a semiconical shape similar or identical to the upper part of the cupola. Several grab handles are mounted on the sides and rear of the cupola. Two M60s are mounted in the rear of the fighting compartment. *US Army Ordnance TSF*

The cupola is traversed to the left in this overhead view of the XM733E1. A close inspection of the photo discloses that the cupola was supported by a flange bolted to the rear of the engine compartment, and by two brackets bolted to the sides of the fighting compartment. A gunner's seat with a back is visible in the rear of the cupola. The M1919 .30-caliber machine gun in the forward station was fed by a flex chute from an ammo box, diagonally mounted in the right side of the compartment. *US Army Ordnance TSF*

The XM733E1 is seen from the rear, showing more of the shape of the turret, which is traversed toward the front. A tow pintle is below the tailgate, and a taillight assembly is to each side of the tailgate. *US Army Ordnance TSF*

A frontal view of the XM733E1 shows the glass vision blocks to each side of the 40 mm automatic grenade launcher. The turret is traversed slightly to the right. Bits of the lower hull of the original M116 cargo carrier are visible around the light armor plates. *US Army Ordnance TSF*

An M116 from the Husky Platoon, 11th Motor Transport Battalion, 1st Marine Division, comes over an embankment while helping villagers harvest crops in the Republic of Vietnam in March 1970. The crew has hung a New Jersey license plate over the section of spare track on the bow. As also can be seen in the next photo, the pioneer tools, including a shovel, ax, and mattock, are stored to the front of the windshield. *National Archives and Records Administration*

In a photo taken on the same occasion as the preceding one, Vietnamese civilians are riding in the cargo compartment of a mud-spattered M116 that is driving into a slough. The number "29" is stenciled on the cab roof to the front of the radio antenna. To the rear is an M116-based XM733 assault vehicle, followed by another M116. The XM733 is armed with an M60 machine gun in the front and a .50-caliber M2 HB machine gun in the rear. *National Archives and Records Administration*

An M116 assigned to Husky Platoon, 11th Motor Transport Battalion, 1st Marine Division, USMC registration no. 346458, is moving across sandy ground while assisting Vietnamese farmers bring in their crops during March 1970. The track shroud is not the Hydrovane type usually associated with the M116. *National Archives and Records Administration*

Marines of 11th Motor Transport Battalion are preparing to load what appears to be a pig in a burlap bag in the straw-filled cargo compartment of an M116 in March 1970. Three ARVN (Army of the Republic of Vietnam) troops are in the cargo compartment. The USMC registration no. 346446 is on the upper right of the tailgate. *National Archives and Records Administration*

Some of the M733 armored Huskies were armed with 81 mm mortars, mounted in the rear of the fighting compartment. These Marines from the 11th Motor Transport Battalion are evidently conducting firing practice toward the ocean from a position near Marble Mountains, on the southeastern outskirts of Da Nang, on March 29, 1970. *National Archives and Records Administration*

A final March 1970 photo of the mission by Husky Platoon, 11th Motor Transport Battalion, to assist local farmers gather their harvest depicts an XM733 armored Husky, USMC registration no. 346497. It is armed with a .50-caliber M2 HB machine gun with a flash suppressor, on a skate rail, and an M60 machine gun. *National Archives and Records Administration*

Some details of the .50-caliber machine gun installation are in view in an 11th Motor Transport Battalion XM733 armored Husky, USMC registration no. 346498. The gun is on a ring mount, evidently a US Navy type, supported by a frame. A conical flash suppressor is on the muzzle of the machine gun. Pioneer tools are secured below the tailgate. *National Archives and Records Administration*

Marines from two units, Husky Platoon, 11th Motor Transport Battalion, and 2nd Battalion, are putting an XM733 armored Husky through its paces in a series of 180- and 360-degree turns on a sand track near Marble Mountains on April 30, 1970. USMC registration no. 346508 is visible on the side. The vehicle is equipped with a skate rail for a machine gun. A "5" bridge-classification sign is on the bow. *National Archives and Records Administration*

CHAPTER 3
The LVTP5 Family of Vehicles

As World War II drew to a close, the military was reevaluating its amphibious tractors. The outgrowth of those efforts was the LVTP5. The Bureau of Ships awarded the Ingersoll Products Division of Borg-Warner a design-and-development contract in December 1950, and the following month work began on the project. The first production pilot of an LVTP5 series vehicle drove off the Kalamazoo, Michigan, assembly line on August 14, 1951.

Additional production contracts were awarded to other firms, including FMC, by then corporately renamed Food, Machinery and Chemical Corp. from the former name Food Machinery Corporation. The first production vehicle drove off the Riverside, California, FMC assembly line and was turned over to the Marines on November 1, 1952.

In addition to Ingersoll and FMC, other firms involved in LVTP5 production included Baldwin-Lima-Hamilton, Pacific Car and Foundry, and St. Louis Car Co.

Stretching over 30 feet in length, the LVTP5 was much larger than its predecessors. The front of the hull formed an inverted-V shape. The inverted-V design was much more efficient in the water than the ramp designs used on earlier LVTs. Despite the shape, the ramp could be lowered for loading and unloading cargo or troops. In addition, on the roof of the vehicle was a large hatch and two smaller ones providing access to the cargo compartment as an alternate means of loading and unloading the vehicle. The vehicle, which had a three-man crew, could transport thirty-four infantry troops on the ground, or twenty-five during water operation.

The crew and passenger compartment was at the front of the vehicle, with the driver's position at the front above the left track channel. On the opposite side was the vehicle commander's station. A machine gun cupola was available, which could be installed at the front of the vehicle between the driver's and commander's hatches.

The power plant was located at the rear of the vehicle, and two more small roof hatches provided access to the engine compartment.

The LVTP5 vehicle tracks were made with inverted grousers in order to propel the vehicle while it was in water. These grousers also served as center guide teeth for the track. The road wheels on the LVTP5 were mounted in pairs, with the center guide teeth running between them. This arrangement meant that each LVTP5 used thirty-six road wheels per track. One wheel of each pair was of conventional design, with a solid rubber tire mounted on a metal wheel. Under normal circumstances, the rubber tire bore the weight of the vehicle. The other wheel was steel rimmed and absorbed shock loads and heavy loads.

By the time production of the LVTP5 ceased in 1957, a total of 1,124 LVTP5s had been completed.

However, fifty-eight of these were subsequently converted to LVTP5 (CMD) vehicles. The genesis of these vehicles was in the LVTCRX1, which itself did not enter production. The vehicle was equipped with racks of radios above the port sidetrack channel and in front of the transverse bulkhead. Radio operators sat on troop seats and stools.

Although production had begun in 1952, the LVTP5 was not deployed until 1956 due to power train and suspension problems. Because the LVTP5 used a transmission that had originally been developed for the M47/M48 tanks, a drop-gear assembly was required to connect the transmission to the final drives, which were positioned about 3 feet lower than the units on tanks. Initially, these drop-gear units and final drives were prone to failure. Modifications to those units to correct these problems, as well the addition of top deck ventilators and snorkels, resulted in the new classification of LVTP5A1 being assigned to these improved vehicles. Externally, the two models can be differentiated by the A1's large housing on the vehicle's rear roof above the engine, which the LVTP5 lacks.

The Ingersoll Products Division of Borg-Warner was awarded a contract in 1951 to build new amphibious vehicles to replace the LVT amtracs of World War II vintage. The first pilot, completed in August 1951, was designated the LVTHX1; the letter "H" referred to its being armed with a howitzer. In this view of the LVTHX1, the bow is to the left, with the driver's cupola to the front of the turret. The hull was constructed of armor up to ⅝ inch thick, with interior structural reinforcing. Toward the rear on each sponson was a prominent radiator air-outlet grille, while an escape hatch was near the center of each sponson. *Chun Hsu*

LVTH6

The LVTH6 was the fire support version of the LVTP5 landing vehicle. The hulls of both types of vehicles were identical, but the LVTH6 had a turret armed with a 105 mm howitzer. The turret was installed over the cargo compartment in the area where the LVTP5's upper cargo hatches were located. The vehicle commander, gunner, and loader were located in the turret, which was equipped with power traverse and main gun elevation. There were two hatches in the turret, one for the commander and one for the loader.

It was mentioned earlier in this chapter that the first production pilot of the LVTP5 series was completed in Kalamazoo in August 1951. That vehicle was an LVTH6. After additional testing, series production of the LVTH6 began in 1954, in Kalamazoo, with the turrets being produced by Wausau Manufacturing Company in Wausau, Wisconsin. Ultimately, 210 LVTH6 howitzer-armed tractors were built, with many being updated to LVTH6A1 configuration.

LVTR1

LVTR1 was developed in 1954 to act as a recovery and maintenance variant of the LVTP5 family. Equipment for this role included a 60,000-pound-capacity drag winch, a separate hoist winch, a 5

cfm air compressor, and a General Electric welder, which were installed in the cargo compartment. The welder could also be used as a battery charger to slave-start other vehicles. The drag winch was powered by a Willys four-cylinder, 48-horsepower MD engine of the type used in the M38A1 quarter-ton Jeep. This engine was also mounted in the cargo compartment. A boom was mounted on the front of the vehicle, which could be erected and used for ordnance maintenance and materials handling. The crew chief acted as the crane operator. The boom had a capacity of 8,000 pounds when used with a single line or 14,000 pounds when rigged with a two-part line.

Once again, modifications were made to the engine's air intake and exhaust system, the vehicle becoming the LVTR1A1.

LVTE1

Like many families of tactical vehicles, the LVTP5 family had an engineer version, known as the LVTE1. It was easily distinguished by its large, toothed, V-shaped excavator blade mounted on the front of the vehicle. This blade could be lowered to the ground and used to clear a 12-foot-wide path through a minefield. Buoyancy tanks were fitted to the rear of the blade, which were filled with plastic foam. This allowed the LVTE1 to maintain level trim when

The LVTHX1 featured a ramp in the bow. The driver's station was in the left side of the bow. Above the driver's station was his cupola; on the opposite side of the vehicle was a cupola for the crew chief. To the front of each cupola were a grab handle and a mooring bitt. Combination headlight assemblies were recessed in the fronts of the sponsons and were equipped with three horizontal brush guards per unit. On production LVTH6s, this headlight arrangement would be replaced by combination headlights on the upper deck. *Chun Hsu*

LVT H6 w/105 How

in the water despite the large appendage. Inside the cargo compartment were two pallets that could be hydraulically raised through the overhead hatches. Each of these pallets carried a rocket-propelled line charge that was also used to clear a path through minefields. Once fired, the used line charge pallet was ejected over the right side of the hull. Like some of the LVTP5s, the LVTE1 mounted a machine gun cupola that was installed between the commander and driver positions.

Late-production LVTE1s were powered by the same Continental AVI-1790-8 twelve-cylinder, fuel-injected gasoline engine as used in the M48A2 tank.

The US Marine Corps was the biggest user of the LVTP5 family of vehicles, although early on the US Army purchased a few examples.

At the time the vehicles began to be issued, Marine amphibious tractor battalions included 120 landing vehicles. This consisted of two tractor companies, each with four platoons encompassing eleven LVTP5A1s. The battalion headquarters was equipped with three LVTP5A1 (CMD) tractors, a maintenance platoon with one LVTR1A1, a mine clearance platoon with eight LVTE1 "potato diggers," and a platoon of twelve LVTP5A1s.

Combat Use

When the 1st and 3rd Marine Divisions deployed to Vietnam in 1965, they took with them the 1st and 3rd Amphibian Tractor Battalions. However, because there were few contested beach landings, the amtracs were commonly used as armored personnel carriers, the same role that the Army used the M113 for. The large and heavy amtracs were not designed for this use, including extensive inland use, which placed unanticipated wear on suspension components. Further, the amtracs had been designed with their fuel tanks on the bottom, which would be submerged during amphibious operations but were vulnerable to land mines when operating inland. The results of driving an LVTP5-series vehicle over an antitank mine were often catastrophic. Famed Marine sniper Carlos Hathcock suffered career-ending third-degree burns pulling fellow Marines from a flame-engulfed LVTP5. Ultimately, it became commonplace for Marines to ride on the outside of the amtracs in Vietnam. While this avoided the danger of being trapped in a flaming box, it negated the armor protection as well.

LVTH6s were often used for direct fire support for Marines, even though they had been designed for indirect fire.

The ramp of the LVTH6 had a triangular indentation on its front, and the bottom of the hull had a similar indentation, running fore and aft. These features improved the stability of the vehicle on water. The steel tracks, 20¾ inches wide, propelled the vehicle in the water. *Chun Hsu*

General Data	
Model	LVTP5
Weight*	87,780
Length**	356
Width**	140.5
Height**	103
Max. speed, land/water	30 mph / 6.8 mph
Fuel capacity	456 gal.
Range	190 miles

* Fighting weight, in pounds
** Overall dimensions listed in inches

Engine Data	
Engine make/model	Continental LV-1790-1
Number of cylinders	12 90-degree V
Cubic-inch displacement	1,790
Horsepower	704 @ 2,800
Torque	1,440 @ 2,000

An LVTH6 is viewed from the left rear, during testing of the vehicle. A white line has been painted around the hull at the waterline. On the lower center of the rear of the hull is a tow hitch with a quick-release mechanism, to which a tow cable is attached. To the left of the tow hitch is the door for the external intercom box. Stern lights are in recesses in the upper corners of the rear of the hull.

"WHEN HORN SOUNDS STAND CLEAR OF RAMP" is painted on the bow of this LVTH6. Faintly visible above the diamond-tread deck inside the vehicle, below the turret, is the forward storage rack for 105 mm ammunition.

A Marine Corps photo dated June 1965 shows a much-smaller warning sign on the bow of an LVTH6A1: "STAND CLEAR OF RAMP." The USMC registration no. 105518 is painted in yellow on the left side of the bow and on the sponson adjacent to the driver's cupola. A short tow cable is attached to the ramp and to a shackle on the towing eye on the bottom of the bow. The LVTH6A1 differed visually from the LVTH6 principally in the presence of a superstructure on the rear deck, for the engine-air intake and exhaust.

This LVTH6A1, USMC registration no. 105595, is parked at the Camp Del Mar area of Camp Pendleton, California. Three recessed boarding steps are arranged one over the other on the center of the side of the vehicle. The center and top steps have a grab handle across them. The single recess to the front of the top step houses the fire-extinguisher activating handle.

This LVTH6A1 is on outdoor display at Camp Pendleton, California. Its USMC registration number is 129053. The 105 mm howitzer tube is secured in the travel lock on the top deck. To the front of the driver's cupola is the left driving-light assembly, with a curved brush guard over it. The triangular indentation in the ramp, to improve stability when underway in water, is visible. *Chris Hughes*

The LVTH6A1 presents the boxy shape of its hull from the left side. To the rear of the turret is the superstructure containing the engine-air inlet and exhaust systems. *Chris Hughes*

In a view of the front part of the left suspension, to the left is the idler, followed by three bogie-wheel assemblies. Each of the nine bogie-wheel assemblies on each side of the vehicle consisted of a pair of hubs, each of which had one steel rim and one demountable solid-rubber-tired rim. The rubber-tired usually carried the load, and the steel rims dealt with heavy-shock loads. On the inside of each track shoe was a grouser, which also served as a track guide. *Chris Hughes*

The three rear bogies and the sprocket on the left side of the LVTH6A1 are displayed. The bogie wheels were mounted on torsion arms. The armored side skirt welded to the bottom of the sponson formed a track channel, which housed the torsion arms, the track-support rollers (five per side), drive sprockets, idler, and track-return skids. *Chris Hughes*

On each sponson was an escape hatch, which could be jettisoned using a quick-release mechanism inside the door. To the front of the hatch are two of the recessed boarding steps, with handgrips. *Chris Hughes*

The radiator air-outlet grilles (the right one is shown) consisted of five sections of steel louvers, which were attached to the hull with bolts. The radiators, behind the grilles, were cooled by engine-powered fans when operating on land. When operating in water, the lower two-thirds of the radiators were underwater, so the driver had to turn off the fans, and cooling was effected by the immersion of the radiators in water. *Chris Hughes*

The LVTH6A1 is viewed from the front right. Details of the sponson, escape hatch, boarding steps, suspension, and radiator grille are the same as on the left side of the vehicle. *Chris Hughes*

The vehicle is observed from the left front. To each side of the ramp is a reinforced towing eye. A single towing eye is on the lower front of the hull, below the ramp. *Chris Hughes*

The fully traversible turret is viewed from the rear. On the rear of the structure is a pioneer tool rack. On the roof are, *left to right*, the loader's hatch, the travel lock for a .50-caliber machine gun, a pedestal mount for a machine gun (near the front of the top deck), and the cupola. The cupola had a dome-shaped hatch door, equipped with four M17 short periscopes and one M17C tall periscope. On the left side of the turret is, *front*, a pistol port, and, *rear*, a vision block. Another vision block is out of view to the front of the pistol port. One vision block, not visible here, is on the right side of the turret, as well as the radio antenna. *Chris Hughes*

The M49 105 mm howitzer tube is viewed from the upper left; it is clamped in its travel lock. The howitzer is installed on the T172 mount. In the foreground, on the left side of the howitzer rotor shield, is the armored shroud for the barrel of the M1919A4E1 .30-caliber coaxial machine gun. *Chris Hughes*

The driver's cupola and the crew chief's cupola (*shown, with the turret to the left*) each had four M17 short-type periscopes and one long-type periscope, mounted individually in steel frames and replaced from inside the vehicle. Bent and welded steel rods serve as deflectors to protect the cupola and periscopes from the howitzer barrel. To the lower right is the front-right bilge-pump outlet; adjacent to it is a lifting eye. *Chris Hughes*

The arrangement of the driver's cupola is similar to that of the crew chief. To the rear of the cupola is the front-left bilge-pump outlet. Toward the right is the forward vision block on the left side of the turret. *Chris Hughes*

On the rear deck, as seen from the left rear of the turret, in the foreground are howitzer deflectors, an antenna mount, and the oblong fighting-compartment hatch. On the center of the deck is the superstructure, containing the engine-air inlet and exhaust outlet, to the sides of which are radiator air-intake grilles. Toward the rear of the deck are two hatches for accessing the engine compartment; the left one is in view. *Chris Hughes*

The rear deck of the LVTH6A1 is observed from the right rear of the turret. At the rear corner of the deck are a lifting eye, a mooring bitt, and the right engine-compartment access hatch. *Chris Hughes*

On the upper corners of the rear of the hull of the LVTH6A1 are recesses for the stern lights, as the taillights are referred to in technical publications. In the left recess are, *left*, a stern light, and, *right*, a blackout stoplight. In the right recess is the right stern light. The vertical channel above the tow hitch contains the quick release for the tow hitch. To the left of the tow hitch is the external interphone-compartment door. The inverted-V shape of the bottom of the hull is discernible. *Chris Hughes*

The front of the hull, including the ramp, and the front of the turret are displayed. The large, round opening to the lower right of the 105 mm howitzer is for the gunner's direct sight. The smaller hole on the opposite side of the rotor shield is the aperture for the M1919A4E1 .30-caliber coaxial machine gun. *Chris Hughes*

Following close on the introduction of the LVTH6 was the "Landing Vehicle, Tracked, Personnel, Mark 5," or LVTP5, amphibious personnel and cargo carrier. It was nearly identical to the LVTH6, except that in lieu of the turret, howitzer, and related systems, the center part of the hull contained a spacious cargo compartment with two bifolding overhead doors. The vehicle commander had his station under the right cupola, opposite the driver's cupola. This newly completed LVTP5 is seen from the right side at the Ingersoll Products plant at Kalamazoo, Michigan. *USMC*

A brand-new LVTP5 has just arrived by flatcar from the Ingersoll Products plant to the Marine Corps Supply Depot, Ordnance Supply Section, Camp Lejeune, North Carolina. Sealant material has been applied over the radiator air-outlet grille and the actuating handle for the fixed fire extinguisher. Along the side of the top deck are toe rails. *USMC*

The large, boxy structure of the LVTP5 lent itself to experimental and operational modifications, such as this example with twin machine guns installed on the top deck. These appear to have been operated remotely from below, since grips and other mechanisms are visible just below the ceiling. Ultimately, an option for a small turret with a single machine gun was available on the LVTP5. Marines are seated in the driver's and vehicle commander's seats. On the center of the transverse bulkhead in the rear of the cargo compartment is the access door to the engine compartment. *USMC*

Several manufacturers produced LVTP5s: Ingersoll, Baldwin-Lima-Hamilton, Pacific Car and Foundry, FMC, and St. Louis Car Company. This sequence of photos documents LVTP5 production at St. Louis Car Company, St. Charles, Missouri. *To the left*, hull assemblies are under assembly on rotary jigs. The second hull in line has been rotated so that the bottom, with its V shape, is in view. *To the right*, assembled hulls are lined up. In the foreground, the driver's cupola and the opening for a machine gun turret are in view. *Washington University*

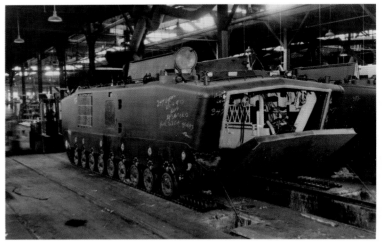

Inspection markings dated March 18 and 19, 1957, have been chalked on the hull of an LVTP5 on the assembly line. The cargo hatch doors have been secured in an upright position. Inside the vehicle, the driver's station and, immediately behind it, the AN/GRC-7 radio set and its X-shaped guards are visible. *Washington University*

A power pack is on a trolley, ready for installation in an LVTP5; it is viewed from the left rear. This consisted of a Continental LF-1790-1 V-12 liquid-cooled engine mated to an Allison CD-850-4B cross-drive transmission. On the side of the engine is the left carburetor. The two cylinders mounted laterally above the transmission are the cross-drive oil coolers. *Washington University*

A Continental LF-1790-1 engine, *left*, and an Allison cross-drive transmission are resting on the St. Louis Car Company floor. The cross-drive oil coolers are not mounted on the transmission. The white object to the left is the fan-drive transmission, which will be mounted on the front of the engine. The disc-shaped assembly on the shop bench is the final-drive pump cluster, which will be mounted on the center rear of the transmission. *Washington University*

The driver's station is viewed from the right side. Below the adjustable seat are, *left*, the ramp-control lever, and, *right*, the diamond-tread footrest. To the front of the seat are the hand-throttle lever, the steer and shift control lever, and the instrument panel. To the upper right is a dome light. *Washington University*

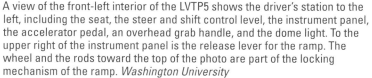

A view of the front-left interior of the LVTP5 shows the driver's station to the left, including the seat, the steer and shift control level, the instrument panel, the accelerator pedal, an overhead grab handle, and the dome light. To the upper right of the instrument panel is the release lever for the ramp. The wheel and the rods toward the top of the photo are part of the locking mechanism of the ramp. *Washington University*

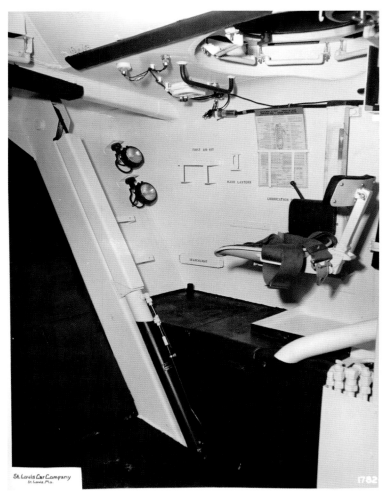

The vehicle commander's station in the right front of the vehicle includes the cupola and periscope brackets (*upper right*), the adjustable seat, and a floor that is part of the top of the right track channel. On the sidewall is a lubrication chart; two service headlights are stored on the front. To the right of the ramp is the right ramp-operating mechanism, including a hydraulic piston, and a cable and sheave (*top*). A corresponding ramp mechanism is also on the left side of the ramp. *Washington University*

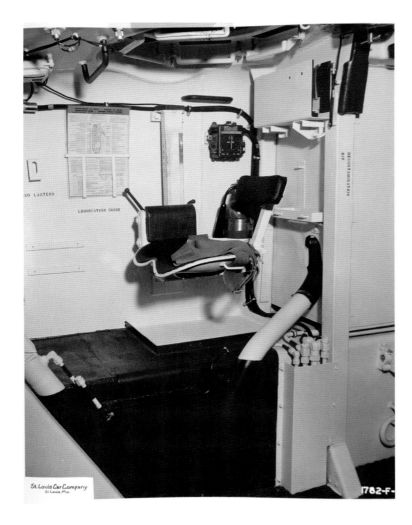

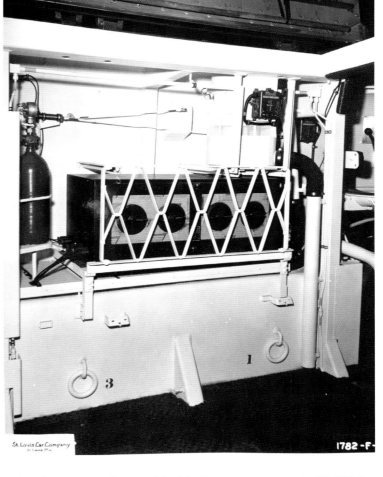

The vehicle commander's station is viewed from a different perspective. Above the seat is an intercom control box. To the right of the seat is a portable fire extinguisher. A decontamination kit is to the upper rear of the seat. *Washington University*

In the left sponson, to the rear of the driver's compartment, are the AN/GRC-7 radio set and its guard. Below the radio are two cargo tie-down rings and two brackets for mounting troop seats. Above the forward end of the radio is the personnel and cargo-compartment ventilating blower. *Washington University*

A substantially completed LVTP5 is near the end of the assembly line. No machine gun turret is present on the low superstructure between the driver's and the vehicle commander's hatches. *Washington University*

In a rear view of an LVTP5 on the St. Louis Car Company assembly line, the recessed stern lights, the quick-release channel above the tow hitch, a grab handle, and five brackets for storing a tow cable are in view. Two toe rails are on the rear of the upper deck; the engine compartment access hatch doors are open. *Washington University*

Although documentation is not available for this photo, it appears to show an LVTP5 undergoing tests of disembarking from a landing-craft ramp. Mooring lines are attached to the bitts on the rear corners of the upper deck. A section of spare track is stored on the deck between the bitts. The raised structure to the front of the spare track is the exhaust vent and muffler outlet. *USMC*

During USMC testing of the LVTP5, a vehicle marked "T6" is engaged in wet loading and unloading with LST-983, off Little Creek, Virginia. Here, the vehicle is about to be wet-loaded on the ramp by means of tow ropes attached to the aft bitts. Bumper tires are secured with ropes to lifting eyes on the top deck. *USMC*

Similar to the LVTH6A1, the LVTP5A1 featured a boxy superstructure toward the rear of the upper deck, visible here on USMC registration no. 107857, above the right radiator grille. It contained the engine-air intake and exhaust systems. *Rock Island Arsenal Museum*

The optional, dome-shaped, fully traversable turret contained five vision blocks, a hatch door, and one M1919A4 .30-caliber machine gun. The turret rested on a low, armored superstructure with two periscopes on the front. To the rear of the turret are the two bifolding cargo hatch doors. Stored on each one is a boarding ladder. To the rear is the superstructure for the engine-air intake and exhaust. *Rock Island Arsenal Museum*

The ramp is lowered on an LVTP5A1, revealing some of the interior. White paint predominates on the interior, with the exception of the deck, which probably was painted Olive Drab. The stencil above the ramp opening reads "WARNING—WHEN HORN SOUNDS—STAND CLEAR." On the inner side of the ramp are two lifting rings, between which is a recessed lug for attaching a chain hoist, for operating the ramp if the hydraulic pistons fail. *Rock Island Arsenal Museum*

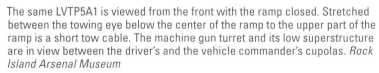

The same LVTP5A1 is viewed from the front with the ramp closed. Stretched between the towing eye below the center of the ramp to the upper part of the ramp is a short tow cable. The machine gun turret and its low superstructure are in view between the driver's and the vehicle commander's cupolas. *Rock Island Arsenal Museum*

A tow cable is dangling from the rear of an LVTP5A1. Details of the rear of the intake/exhaust superstructure are in view. *Rock Island Arsenal Museum*

This LVTP5A1, USMC registration no. 107646, is on display at Camp Pendleton, California. It is armed with a machine gun turret between the driver's and vehicle commander's hatches. *Author*

The LVTP5A1 is observed from the left front. The triangular recess in the front of the ramp is visible in this and the preceding photo. *Chris Hughes*

The armored superstructure for the air intake and the exhaust is prominent in this right-rear view of the LVTP5A1. The quick-release tow hitch toward the lower center of the rear of the hull is visible. *Chris Hughes*

A rear view of the vehicle includes the recessed stern lights, with a blackout stoplight also present in the right side of the left recess. The vertical metal channel that protects the quick-release cable for the tow hitch has a large dent toward the top. *Chris Hughes*

In a view of the rear of the upper deck from the right side, in the center foreground is the right rear hook, for securing the cargo hatch doors (*lower right*) in the open position. To the immediate rear of the hook is the exhaust door for the auxiliary generator, to the inboard side of which is the right entry hatch door. In the background are the right radiator cooling-air intake grille and the superstructure for the air intake and exhaust. *Chris Hughes*

As seen from the left side of the upper deck, facing aft, in the center foreground is the right rear cargo-door hook, in the lowered position. Just beyond it is the left entry hatch. *Chris Hughes*

The machine gun turret is viewed from the left side of the cargo hatch. To the lower left is one of four cargo-compartment vents, to the front of which is the driver's cupola. *Chris Hughes*

The turret is viewed from the right side of the cargo hatch, flanked by the two cupolas. In the center foreground is the front hinge of the right cargo-hatch door. *Chris Hughes*

Ingersoll constructed a single pilot LVTAAX1 amphibious tracked antiaircraft vehicle in 1954. Based on an LVTP5 chassis, the LVTAAX1 was armed with a twin 40 mm gun mount, of the type used on the M42 self-propelled twin 40 mm gun. Ammunition for these guns was stored in the cargo compartment and in ready racks around the mount. *Chun Hsu*

The sole pilot LVTAAX1 has survived and is stored at Camp Pendleton, California. The outer, rubber-tired wheels have been removed from several of the bogie-wheel assemblies, including the second and third ones and the two rearmost ones. *Chris Hughes*

The LVTAAX1 is observed from the front left, with the driver's hatch door open. A spare bogie rim with rubber tire is lying next to the driver's cupola. *Chris Hughes*

The twin 40 mm gun mount is viewed from the rear from a position on the upper deck. Along the rear quarter of the mount are lockers for clipped 40 mm ammunition. To the rear of the gun mount is the entry hatch. To the right of that hatch is the door for the auxiliary generator exhaust. *Chris Hughes*

In a photo taken 180 degrees from the perspective of the preceding photo, facing aft on the upper deck of the LVTAAX1, the feature with the expanded-steel mesh at the center is what remains of the exhaust vent and muffler outlet. To the rear are engine-compartment access doors, two mooring bitts, a vent hood, and two toe rails. *Chris Hughes*

Ingersoll developed a command version of the LVTP5 in 1955. These were originally designated the LVTCRX1, but later, command vehicles converted from existing LVTP5 chassis were designated the LVTP5A1 (CMD). These vehicles were equipped with nine radio sets and seating for six operators in the cargo compartment. Additional antennas were mounted on the upper deck. This LVTP5A1, Marine Corps registration no. 107601, is parked in a vehicle yard at Camp Del Mar, part of Camp Pendleton, California, in an undated photo. *USMC*

A machine gun turret is installed on an LVTP5A1 (CMD), Marine Corps registration no. 107994, in a photo dated 1966. The -A1 in the vehicle designation referred to the superstructure toward the rear of the upper deck. *USMC*

Food Machinery and Chemical Company (FMC), a longtime manufacturer of amphibious military vehicles, converted an LVTP5 to a maintenance and recovery vehicle, designated the LVTRX1, in 1954. It featured a winch driven by an engine from an M38A1 ¼-ton truck. The vehicle also was fitted with a boom and General Electric welding equipment. Its designated purposes were vehicular recovery and maintenance (including replacing power packs), but it also was useful for general heavy lifting and dragging. The LVTRX1 entered production, standardized as the "Landing Vehicle, Tracked, Recovery," LVTR1. When equipped with the superstructure on the upper deck for the air intake and exhaust, as seen here on USMC registration no. 120063, the vehicle was designated the LVTR1A1. *Chun Hsu*

An LVTR1A1, registration no. 120063, is observed from the upper left with the boom and kingpost erected. Steel cables act as side braces for the kingpost, and a substantial steel back brace spans from the upper part of the kingpost to a bracket on the upper deck. On the front of the base of the kingpost is the bow fairlead, a swiveling sheave for guiding the winch cable. On the rear of the upper deck was a stern fairlead, not visible here. To the front of the superstructure for the air intake and exhaust on the upper deck is a sliding sheave housing, from which the cables from the retrieving winch and the crane winch are paid out. Faintly visible inside the hull is a dark-colored, diagonal structure, the top of which is below the kingpost: this was a compression strut. The crane operator's station was to the left of the strut, above the track channel. An anvil is mounted on the right side of the ramp; a chain is attached to the ramp for manual operation, since the cables for hydraulic operation have been disconnected. *Chun Hsu*

A view into the open ramp door of an LVTR1 or LVTRA1 during a 1st Marine Division exercise in the Mojave Desert in California shows oxygen and acetylene bottles secured to the compression strut. To the far right in the photo, part of the driver's seat and seat belt are visible. In the background, a crewman seated on a bogie wheel is operating the radio. In the center and the rear of the compartment are the winch power unit, the retrieving and the crane winches, air compressors, and other fixtures. *USMC*

This LVTR1A1, USMC registration no. 120064, is preserved at Camp Pendleton, California. The crane is stored it its travel position. Above the top center of the ramp is the bow fairlead, with the end of a recovery cable protruding from it. *Chris Hughes*

The two rings welded to the upper corners of the bow were for securing cables or chains to control the position of the boom with reference to the fore-and-aft centerline of the vehicle. *Chris Hughes*

The bow fairlead, manufactured by Berger, incorporates a sheave on a swiveling mount, to direct the recovery cable to the front as needed. The link above the fairlead is the kingpost-erecting strut. *Chris Hughes*

In a view of the top of the bow from the right side, to the far right is the right eye for securing the boom. To its immediate rear are the bracket and turnbuckle for the right stay cable for the kingpost; one end of the steel cable is attached to the turnbuckle, and the other end to the kingpost. To the left is the crane operator's cupola. *Chris Hughes*

As seen from the center of the left side of the hull of the LVTR1A1, the boom of the crane, in its travel position, rests on a support attached to the upper deck. Two sheaves are on the end of the boom. On the hull, to the left is the recess for the pull handle for the fixed fire extinguisher; to the right is the upper step. *Chris Hughes*

The bow fairlead is viewed from the left side. To its rear, in their travel positions, are, *top to bottom*, the kingpost, the boom, and the back brace of the kingpost. *Chris Hughes*

The kingpost, the back brace, and the boom are observed from the right side of the upper deck, facing forward. The recovery cable is visible as it proceeds forward to the fairlead. *Chris Hughes*

As seen from the left side of the upper deck, with the crane boom at the lower left, to the left of center is the bracket to which the bottom of the back brace is fastened. On the top of the bracket is a rest for the kingpost. The back brace consists of two pieces, pinned in the center. When the crane is erected, the two pieces of the back brace form a straight line; when the crane is lowered, the back brace collapses into a V shape, as seen below the kingpost to the left. *Chris Hughes*

Seen from the left side of the upper deck, facing aft, at the center is the housing for the sliding sheave. To the side of the housing are a cam lock for the cargo door and a crew hatch. To the rear is the air intake and exhaust superstructure. In the foreground are the severely corroded cargo doors and a pioneer tool rack. *Chris Hughes*

The LVTR1A1 at Camp Pendleton is seen from the left rear, showing the relative positions of the lowered crane, the housing for the sliding sheave, and the superstructure. A quick-release tow hitch is on the rear of the hull. *Chris Hughes*

Based on the LVTP5 chassis, a single pilot LVTEX1 engineer vehicle was completed in 1955. Its principal purposes were to clear minefields and convey engineers and their equipment. It mounted a sizable excavator blade on the bow, for clearing ground or mines. The production version, LVTE1, as seen in this photo of registration no. 106035, had the air-cooled AVI-1790-8 engine and thus lacked the radiator grilles on the side. Above the upper deck is the rocket launcher, for propelling line charges: lines with a series of explosive charges attached, for clearing minefields by blowing them up. The excavator blade is partly visible to the right.

In a left-front view of the same LVTE1, registration no. 106035, on the semitrailer the massive excavator blade is in the foreground. It was equipped with triangular teeth on the bottom, to expedite clearing and detonating mines.

The same excavator blade is observed from the front. Wings to the sides of the blade are folded forward. The two halves of the main blade are joined vertically, fastened with bolts, in the center. The excavator was fabricated from steel, with aluminum-alloy teeth.

Two pallets containing a line charge and the rocket that deployed the charge were carried in the cargo compartment of the LVTE1. To fire the line charge, the pallet was raised by hydraulic power into the position shown here. After firing, the pallet was jettisoned over the side. This vehicle has the Continental LV-1790-1 liquid-cooled engine and thus has radiator grilles on the sides. *Chun Hsu*

This LVTE1, registration no. 106005, displays the raised excavator with wings folded forward. Two hydraulic cylinders served to lower and raise the excavator. The brush guard to the front of the USMC registration number on the sponson protected a side periscope. To the rear of the machine gun turret are the line-charge rocket launcher and the cargo hatch. Visible on the upper rear of the excavator are two cells, filled with air and plastic foam, to assist with flotation of the excavator during waterborne operations. *Chun Hsu*

The buoyancy cells on the upper rear of the excavator are readily seen in this frontal view of an LVTE1. The bent plate at the front of the rocket launcher was a combination launcher support and shield. The ramp on the bow was eliminated and was replaced by a new structure that bulged outward, instead of having a triangular recess on it. *Chun Hsu*

The teeth of the excavator presented a fearful aspect. Their idea was to detonate or plow up mines without dropping the excavator blade into the ground. *Chun Hsu*

The impressive LVT collection at Camp Pendleton, California, includes this example of an LVTE1, registration no. 138057. The original escape hatch on the side of the sponson was welded shut, and a new escape hatch with two hinges and a visor was installed farther forward. The low, accordion-shaped structure on the upper deck aft of the rocket launcher was the armor cover plate for the cooling-air intake valve; an identical one is on the opposite side of the upper deck. *Chris Hughes*

The hydraulic cylinders for operating the excavator have been removed, but the support arms and the buoyancy cells of the excavator are visible. In addition to the standard steps to the rear of the new escape hatch, two new steps were cut into the skirt below the hatch. *Chris Hughes*

The LVTE1 at Camp Pendleton is viewed from the front, showing details of the excavator, its teeth and buoyancy cells, and the wings to the side. The upper part of the revised bow is in view. Inboard of the locations for the hydraulic pistons are two latches for securing the excavator blade when raised. *Chris Hughes*

A close-up view of the front of the excavator shows how the two blade-and-teeth assemblies are bolted together at the center. *Chris Hughes*

A right-front view of the excavator depicts the buoyancy cells and the folded right wing. *Chris Hughes*

The excavator of the LVTE1 is observed from the right rear, showing the arms (which are resting on a wooden beam) and the rears of the buoyancy cells. Two small access holes, the right one of which lacks its cover plate, are at the tops of the cells. *Chris Hughes*

During a training exercise at Quantico, Virginia, an LVTP5 numbered "12" is coming ashore as Marines in the background assault a pillbox with a flamethrower. A dark-colored stripe is painted on the vehicle to the front of the escape hatch. The Marine Corps released this photo for publication on January 16, 1956, so, judging by the deciduous trees in the background that are bare of leaves, it was taken not long before that date. *USMC*

In an aerial photo taken at Quantico, Marines delivered to a beach from three LVTP5s are advancing against fortified positions during an amphibious training exercise. The nearest vehicle has a white number "13" on the hull below the driver's cupola. *USMC*

Marines from Company K, 3rd Battalion, 6th Marines, have taken prone positions on the beach in front of LVTP5A1s that have just landed at Onslow Beach, Camp Lejeune, North Carolina, on December 22, 1960. These vehicles possess the air-intake and exhaust superstructure that was a key feature of the -A1 version of the vehicle. The vehicles are numbered in yellow "2B11" (*left*) and "2B10." Both have machine gun turrets. *USMC*

Cpl. Bobby D. Routh, of the 1st Amphibian Tractor Battalion, plays Santa Claus next to an LVTP5A1 that has been painted white and decorated, Christmas style, at a Christmas party at Camp White Beach on Okinawa, around 1960.

Amid explosions, troops from the 2nd Marine Division are storming ashore from LVTP5As at Onslow Beach, Camp Lejeune, in February 1964. The two visible vehicles have machine turrets without the guns installed. *USMC*

Members of the 2nd Battalion, 3rd Marine Regiment, 3rd Marine Division, are firing a 106 mm recoilless rifle mounted on the upper deck of an LVTP5A1 during a sweep-and-clear operation near the Ca De Song River on August 13, 1965. The code "B 34" is painted on the ramp, and the nickname "HOTEL" is visible on the left side of the top of the bow. *National Archives*

The LVTP5A1 saw extensive service in Southeast Asia with the Marine Corps during the Vietnam War. In this photo taken from above the cargo hatch of an LVTP5A1, the vehicle commander is standing in his cupola hatch, giving hand signals, while three other LVTP5A1s stand by, partially in the water, along the beach in the background. *National Archives*

An LVTP5A1 from Company B, 3rd Amtrac Battalion, registration no. 108151, escorts members of Company H, 2nd Battalion, 3rd Marines, during a sweep-and-clear mission along the Ca De Son River on August 13, 1965. The vehicle is marked "B 38" on the ramp and over the side escape hatch. *National Archives*

On day two of a two-day sweep-and-clear mission to eradicate Vietcong fighters around the village of Pho Thuong Ho, Republic of Vietnam, on August 13, 1965, Marines from the 2nd Battalion, 3rd Marines, are advancing along a road, accompanied by an LVTP5 or LVTP5A1 in the distance. In addition to providing transport and firepower for the troops, these vehicles also transported local civilians who wished to evacuate the dangerous area. *National Archives*

Marines from Company B, 2nd Battalion, 3rd Marines, are firing a 106 mm recoilless rifle mounted on the upper deck of the previously depicted LVTP5A1 nicknamed "HOTEL" and numbered "B 34." This was during a three-day operation in the Elephant Valley, 12 miles west of the Da Nang Airbase, on August 19, 1965. Another amtrac is in the background. *National Archives*

At the Marine Aircraft Group 12 (MAG-12) base at Chu Lai on October 22, 1965, the crew of an LVTP5A1 that was converted to a crash vehicle stands by, awaiting any emergency calls. The crew nicknamed this vehicle the "Amcrash," a combination of "amtrac" and "crash" vehicle. Outfitted with firefighting and rescue gear, the Amcrash was handy at this airbase in responding to emergency situations in the sandy soil around the base, which proved difficult for crash trucks to drive on. *National Archives*

Sandbags have been arranged for crew protection atop the forward end of the upper deck of this LVTP5A1, registration no. 107545, during the landing of elements of the 3rd Marine Division during Operation Piranha, an offensive against the 1st Vietcong Regiment on the Patangan Peninsula, Quang Ngai Province, Republic of Vietnam, from September 7 to 10, 1965. *National Archives*

Grunts from the 3rd Marine Division are assembling prior to a sweep against Vietcong forces next to an LVTP5A1 marked "1-A-21" during 1965. On the escape hatch is a yellow, shield-shaped battalion marking, the details of which are illegible. *National Archives*

Members of Company E, 2nd Battalion, 1st Marine Regiment, are disembarking from an LCM-8 "Mike Boat" mechanized landing craft on the Song Tu Bong River while an LVTH6A1 awaits in the background, in August 1966. The Marines were preparing to set up a perimeter for an overnight bivouac for Operation Swanee. *National Archives*

A column of LVTP5A1s are preparing to move out with troops of the 1st Marine Division during the kickoff of Operation Arcadia on November 14, 1966. The vehicle in the foreground marked "A20" below the machine gun turret bears registration no. 108470 on the left side of the bow; below it is a battalion shield. *National Archives*

Several Marines with portable radio sets were photographed around a pair of LVTP5A1s from the 1st Amtrac Battalion during 1966. Registration no. 107674 is painted in yellow on the bow of the closer amtrac. Sandbags are carefully stacked to form a shield on the forward part of the upper deck of the other vehicle. *National Archives*

Members of 1st Amtrac Battalion are laying down mortar fire on an enemy position, while their LVTP5A1, marked "B 40" on the rear, is parked in the background, in Vietnam around 1966. This is the same vehicle as the one in the background in the preceding photograph, with sandbags stacked on the forward part of the upper deck and two oil drums secured to the sides of the deck.

An LVTH6A1 marked "26" is being backed into position for a wet loading onto the ramp of USS *Coconino County* (LST-603) at Subic Bay, Philippine Islands, on January 4, 1967. The ship and the amtrac were about to depart for South Vietnam for landings in the Mekong delta for the start of Operation Deckhouse Five. *National Archives*

A pair of 105 mm howitzer-armed LVTH6A1s are chugging through the water of the South China Sea off the Mekong delta during Operation Deckhouse Five, a joint USMC–Republic of Vietnam Marine Corps sweep of the delta from January 6 to 15, 1967. The closer amtrac is marked "21" on the sponson. *National Archives*

Marines of 2nd Battalion, 5th Marines, 1st Marine Division, are positioned behind an embankment, with an amtrac in the foreground and an LVTE1 engineer amtrac in the background, during Operation New Castle, on March 6, 1967. The dozer of the LVTE1 has been in recent use, since the wings are extended and soil and grass are on the blade and the teeth. *National Archives*

Two LVTE1s from the 1st Amphibian Tractor Battalion are on the advance during Operation Perry in the Republic of Vietnam on March 24, 1967. The closer engineer amtrac has an ace of spades on the front of the sponson and the number "3 H 25" on the upper center of the sponson. What appears to be a tiger's eye is painted on the excavator blade. *National Archives*

Marines from Company F, 2nd Battalion, 5th Marines, are riding on an LVTP5A1, *left,* and an LVTE1 (the excavator is visible on the front of the vehicle), *right,* during a river crossing in Vietnam on March 26, 1967. This was during a search-and-destroy mission code-named Operation New Castle, in Quang Nam Province. The LVTP5A1 is marked "32 A 38" on the rear. *National Archives*

An LVTP5A1 from the 5th Marine Division are transporting at least fifteen soldiers from the US Army's 196th Light Infantry Brigade, part of Task Force Oregon, in a combined search-and-destroy operation outside Chu Lai in April 1967. The vehicle bears USMC registration no. 108459. The vehicle commander and the driver are in their cupola hatches and are wearing combat-vehicle crewman (CVC) helmets. *National Archives*

An LVTE1 is serving as a battle taxi, transporting marines of the 1st Marine Division across a rice paddy during Operation Elliot "A" in Vietnam on July 7, 1967. The object wedged between the excavator blade and the bow of the vehicle is a pallet for an M58 high-explosive demolition line charge. Tiger eyes are painted on the blade. *National Archives*

Republic of Vietnam (RVN) soldiers are unloading boxes of ammunition from an LVTP5A1, registration no. 107428, assigned to Company B, 1st Amphibian Tractor Battalion, 3rd Marine Division, by the mouth of the Cua Viet River on October 2, 1967. Sandbags are piled up to protect a .30-caliber machine gun on the upper deck. *National Archives*

An LVTH6A1 is conducting a fire mission with its 105 mm howitzer at an undisclosed location in the Republic of Vietnam on January 31, 1968. Ammunition packing tubes are stacked in the foreground. To the rear of the turret, the crew hatch is open. *National Archives*

A column of LVTP5s or LVTP5A1s are approaching the ramp of the amphibious transport dock USS *Austin* (LPD-4) during maneuvers in Roosevelt Roads, Puerto Rico, on June 18, 1968. A wooden crate is stored to the rear of the machine gun turret on the closest amtrac. *National Archives*

An LVTE1 from the Battalion Landing Team, 2nd Battalion, 7th Marines, 3rd Marine Division, is on a mission to secure a road during a Special Landing Force operation in Quang Nam Province, about 20 miles south of Da Nang, Republic of Vietnam, on August 15, 1968. Extensive sandbag protection has been added to the forward end of the upper deck. The wings are absent from the excavator. *National Archives*

A Marine is "walking" an LVTP5A1, registration no. 108480, at the base near the Marble Mountains in 1968. "Walking" a vehicle was a safety practice, to prevent Marines on foot from inadvertently venturing into the path of an advancing vehicle. Under the cover above the sandbag emplacement on the amtrac is an M2 HB .50-caliber machine gun. *National Archives*

An LVTH6A1 is plowing into the surf at the China Sea Rest and Recreation Center, 4 miles southeast of Da Nang, as part of an amphibious convoy to the town of Hoi An, near the mouth of the Thu Bon River, on March 3, 1969. An armored shield is on the .50-caliber machine gun mount on top of the turret. *USMC*

The 105 mm howitzer of an LVTH6A1 from the 1st Marine Division has just been fired during a support mission for ground troops during Operation Oklahoma Hills in Vietnam on April 15, 1969. The vertical tube near the front of the turret roof is the panoramic telescope, used in indirect fire. In the foreground is a sandbag revetment, for the protection of the side of the amtrac. *National Archives*

The crane of an LVTR1 maintenance and recovery amtrac, *right*, is pulling the power pack from an LVTP5A1, registration no. 107506, at a Marine Corps base near the Marble Mountains, sometime in 1968. On the sponson of the LVTR1 are the nickname "Call Girl" and corresponding artwork. *National Archives*

At the unidentified base of an ordnance maintenance company, part of a maintenance battalion, in the Republic of Vietnam in 1969, an LVTR1 crane is being used to hoist reconditioned power packs into a row of amtracs. Each power pack comprises a Continental LV-1790-1 V-12 engine and an Allison CD-850-4B transmission.

US Marine Corps LVTP5A1 amtracs are returning to the tank landing ship USS *Newport* (LST-1179) during Exercise Exotic Dancer III, in the Atlantic Ocean in May 1970. One of the vehicles is ascending the ramp, while another one waits its turn. *USMC*

The crewmen of a USMC LVTP5A1, registration no. 108156, are in their hatches while underway in the Atlantic Ocean during Exercise Exotic Dancer III on May 18, 1970. The code "C10" is painted in yellow above the registration number on the sponson. *USMC*

LVTP5A1s from the 4th Marine Division are cruising abreast during a rehearsal landing at White Beach, Camp Pendleton, California, on August 16, 1970. This was during a training exercise called Operation High Desert. *USMC*

Four LVTP5A1s are maneuvering toward White Beach at Camp Pendleton on August 16, 1970. On the nearest amtrac, the vertical tube just behind the open crew hatch door is a fuel-filler extension, used for filling the fuel tanks while the vehicle is afloat. *USMC*

Marines are hitting the beach, delivered by an LVTP5A1 code-numbered 3-B-14, at Camp Pendleton during Operation High Desert, on August 17, 1970. The left mooring bit on the top of the bow is painted red, while the right one is white. *USMC*

CHAPTER 4
The LVTP7/AAV7A1-Series Vehicles

By 1964, the LVTP5 was nearing the end of its projected fifteen-year service life, and accordingly the Marines issued a requirement for a successor. Among the firms responding were Chrysler and, not surprisingly, FMC. In 1966, FMC was awarded the development contract.

The new vehicle, which during development was designated LVTPX12, like the LVTP5, would be completely enclosed, but whereas the LVTP5 body was steel, the new vehicle utilized 5083 aluminum armor, which resulted in a greatly reduced vehicle weight. Notably, the new vehicle used torsion bar suspension, as did most US armored vehicles of the era, rather than the Torsilastic suspension used by all US amtracs since the LVT-2. This change was driven by the extensive inland use of the LVTP5 in Vietnam with the associated accelerated wear on the suspension, which the elastomers in the Torsilastic suspension were ill suited for.

Further, the LVTPX12 drive sprocket was at the front, and the ramp at the rear. This was the opposite layout of the LVTP5. Powering the vehicle was a GM 8V53T engine developing 400 horsepower. The engine was coupled to a four-speed semiautomatic transmission. Rather than using the tracks for propulsion in the water, the LVTP7 used a water jet on either side of the vehicle.

In the summer of 1967, the first of the twelve prototypes of the LVTPX12-series vehicles were completed by FMC. The first machine was a basic LVTPX12. In 1969, the LVTCX2, a command vehicle, was completed, and the next year two LVTRX2 recovery vehicle prototypes were completed.

Both the driver and infantry troop commander were provided with cupolas on the left side of the hull, while the vehicle commander had his own weapon station on the right side of the hull, which was armed with an M139 20 mm gun and a coaxial 7.62 mm machine gun. The assistant driver's position was behind the infantry troop commander. The LVTPX12 had roof hatches to provide overhead access to the cargo compartment.

Troop trials of the new amphibians were conducted from 1967 until June 1970. In 1970 the vehicle was type-classified as the LVTP7, and in May 1970 FMC was awarded a low-rate initial production contract for thirty-eight vehicles, valued at $10.4 million. The next month the firm was awarded a $78.5 million full-rate series production contract. The first production vehicle was delivered on August 26, 1971.

Deliveries of the LVTC7 command vehicles and LVTR7 recovery vehicles began in 1972. Production of the LVTP7-series vehicles was completed in April 1974. By that time, 942 LVTP7s, eighty-four LVTC7s, and fifty-five LVTR7s had been manufactured.

By the early 1980s, the LVTP7 was reaching the end of its planned ten-year service life. After considering various options for a new generation of amphibious tractors, and in view of the excellent performance provided to that point by the LVTP7, a Service Life Extension Program (SLEP) was instituted to remanufacture the vehicles. The SLEP promised to improve the reliability, communications, and safety of the LVTP7. As part of the program, the GM 8V53T engine, used in the original version, was replaced with the Cummins VT400 diesel engine, driving the vehicle through an FMC HS-400-3A1 transmission. The hydraulic systems that powered the weapons were replaced by electric motors, which eliminated the danger from hydraulic-fluid fires. Improvements were made to the suspension and shock absorbers, and the fuel tank was also improved. A fuel-burning smoke generator system was added to the vehicles, as well as eight smoke grenade launchers being mounted around the weapons station.

The Marines processed their remaining inventory of LVTP7s through this program, which included 853 LVTP7 personnel tractors, seventy-seven LVTC7 command tractors, and fifty-four LVTR7 recovery vehicles.

However, additional vehicles were required, and from 1983 through 1985, FMC produced an additional 294 personnel tractors, which were designated LVTP7A1. Also, newly built were twenty-nine LVTC7A1s and ten LVTR7A1s. The headlight recesses were square on these vehicles, compared to the round recesses used previously. The A1 suffix was also added to the older vehicles as they emerged from the SLEP. Inside, an improved instrument panel was installed, as was a night vision device, new fuel tanks, and a new ventilation system.

In 1984, the Marine Corps re-designated the LVTP7A1 as AAVP7A1. The change in designation reflected a change in the role of the vehicle within the Corps, where, in addition to its designed role in amphibious assault with minimal inland use, it would also double as an armored personnel carrier during extensive overland operations.

To meet the additional requirements, a series of modifications were made to the vehicles as part of a Product Improvement Program (PIP), many of which had been under consideration even before the expanded role was developed. Including in the PIP were installation of add-on armor as well as updated radio equipment.

At about the same time, the original cupola-mounted .50-caliber M85 weapon station was replaced with a new system from Cadillac

Twelve pilots of an amtrac personnel and cargo carrier to replace the LVTP5 were produced, with the first one coming off the FMC assembly line in the summer of 1967. Designated the LVTPX12 (the third pilot is depicted), the vehicle had a hull formed of 5083 aluminum armor, and its 21-inch-wide tracks rode on six dual bogie wheels, driven by front sprockets. Propulsion on water was by two water jets on the rears of the sponsons. The engine was mounted in the bow, and the ramp was on the stern. On the left was the driver's cupola, with a cupola for the troop commander to the rear. On the right side was a turret, referred to as the weapon station, with an M139 20 mm cannon and a coaxial M73E1 7.62 mm machine gun. *USMC*

Gage. Dubbed the Up-Gunned Weapon Station, or UGWS, the new turret was armed with both a .50-caliber M2HB machine gun and a 40 mm Mk 19 MOD 3 automatic grenade launcher (AGL).

Despite all of these improvements, by 1986 efforts were being made to further improve the vehicles through enhanced protection. The initial result of this effort was awarding a $2.84 million contract to the Majestic Metal Fabrication Company of Roseville, Michigan, on March 6, 1987. The contract provided for the procurement of 189 appliqué armor kits (AAK) for the Marine Corps' assault amphibious vehicle 7A1 (AAV7A1) personnel and command and control vehicles. The passive standoff armor purchased for the AAV7A1 was the P900 AAK model, consisting of perforated plates attached to the vehicle hull. The AAK would significantly improve AAV7A1 survivability against small-arms kinetic-energy munitions.

In 1989, a new type of appliqué armor began to be procured for the AAV7A1. Known as the enhanced appliqué armor kit (EAAK), the new system was developed by the Israeli firm Rafael Armament Development Authority. Delivery of the kits began in 1991, and by 1993 the Corps had purchased 1,137 sets. While effective at its design objectives, stopping 95 percent of 14.5 mm armor-piercing rounds fired from 400 meters, the kits were subject to damage from saltwater amphibious operations. As a result, additional kits were procured, and fifty-five to seventy-five kits are replaced annually.

Mounting the kits includes first attaching mounting points to the hull. The almost 2-ton weight of the EAAK altered the trim of the vehicle and necessitated the installation of a bow plane as part of the installation process.

The next major upgrade to the venerable amtrac was the Assault Amphibious Vehicle Reliability, Availability, Maintainability / Rebuild to Standard (AAV RAM/RS) Program, which was approved in 1997. This program was intended to return the vehicle to its original performance specifications, despite the significantly increased weight brought on by the various modifications and PIP, as well as the degradation inherent with decades of use.

The AAV RAM/RS program replaced the 400-horsepower Cummins VT400 diesel of the AAV7A1 with a Cummins VTA903T diesel engine developing 525 horsepower. The VTA903T is the engine used in the Bradley Fighting Vehicle. Also taken over from the Bradley as part of the AAV RAM/RS was the suspension system. As a result of these changes, ground clearance, which through weight increases and fatigue had been reduced to less than 12 inches, returned to 16 inches, and the horsepower-to-ton ratio increased from 13:1 to its original 17:1. The increased horsepower required modifications to the transmission, with the improved unit being designated HS-525. During the vehicle upgrade, new United Defense "Big Foot" track was installed. Vehicles processed through the program had a RAM/RS suffix added to their model designations. Initially 680 vehicles were processed through the program, with the first one being turned over to the Marines in 1999 and the last one in 2004. The impressive record of these vehicles during Operation Iraqi Freedom led the Marines to contract for a further 391 vehicles to go through the RAM/RS program, the last of which were completed in 2007.

The LVTP7 had been declared operational on April 5, 1972, when C Company of the 2nd Amphibian Tractor Company began

The LVTPX12 was standardized as the LVTP7 and entered production at FMC, with the first one being delivered in the fall of 1971. On this vehicle, an M60 7.62 mm machine gun is mounted above the weapon station, which normally housed an M85 .50-caliber machine gun; the vehicle commander's head is below the M60. A camouflage net is stowed on the side of the hull. *USMC*

using the vehicles. Soon the 2nd Amphibian Tractor Battalion of the 2nd Marine Division, the 3rd Amphibian Tractor Battalion of the 1st Marine Division, and the 4th Amphibian Tractor Battalion of the 4th Marine Division of the USMC Reserve, along with one company of the 1st Tracked Vehicle Battalion of the 3rd Marine Division, were equipped with the vehicles.

In August 1982, LVTP7s were deployed to a hot zone for the first time when the 2nd Assault Amphibian Battalion deployed as part of the multinational peacekeeping force in Beirut, Lebanon. Used as armored personnel carriers (APCs) in a primarily urban area through February 1983, several of the amtracs sustained minor damage from shrapnel and small-arms fire.

On October 25, 1983, Golf Company, 2nd Battalion, 9th Marine Regiment, used LVTP7s to conduct a very successful amphibious landing on the island of Grenada as part of Operation Urgent Fury.

In 1991, AAV7PA1 amtracs of the 2nd, 3rd, and 4th Assault Amphibian Battalions were used in Operation Desert Storm. The 1st and 2nd Marine Divisions used the vehicles as armored personnel carriers, as well as some vehicles taking part in amphibious landings as a feint.

On December 9, 1992, the 3rd Assault Amphibian Battalion conducted a landing on the shore of Somalia near the Mogadishu International Airport as part of Operation Restore Hope, a UN-led initiative to provide humanitarian aid to the nation, which at that time was torn by civil war.

One of the most inland operations of the AAV7A1 occurred in June 1999, when the 3rd Assault Amphibian Battalion was deployed to Kosovo as part of the NATO mission in Kosovo (KFOR).

During and after the Second Gulf War, the AAV7A1, along with many other US vehicles, was sharply criticized for providing inadequate protection for personnel inside. During the Battle of Nasiriyah, eight of the amtracs were damaged or destroyed by rocket-propelled grenade (RPG) rounds, as well as mortar, tank, and artillery fire, although one was destroyed in a "friendly fire" incident when engaged by an A-10 Warthog attack aircraft.

An August 3, 2005, encounter with an IED (improvised explosive device) left fourteen Marines and an Iraqi interpreter dead and their amtrac destroyed in the city of Haditha in the Euphrates River valley.

But it was not these combat encounters that led to a massive change in the AAV7A1 duty, but rather a training accident.

On July 30, 2020, AAV7A1 serial number 523519, assigned to Battalion Landing Team 1/4, sank off the coast of San Clemente Island, California, during a training exercise, killing eight Marines and a Navy corpsman. The ensuing investigation revealed a myriad of problems, which, in aggregate, led to these deaths. Counter to operational procedures, there was no safety boat on standby, the men who were killed had not received the required underwater evacuation training, according to some reports the sea state was rougher than was permissible for a training exercise, and there was an excessive delay—some suggest over twenty minutes—in ordering the crew to evacuate. Also, a factor was the condition of the AAV7A1, which reportedly had only recently been pulled from a deadline and hastily made ready for the training exercise, during which a transmission failure due to low oil had caused it to go dead in the water, as well as triggering a system designed

The round recesses for the headlights on the bow were an identification feature of the LVTP7, versus the LVTP7A1. On the forward deck, which has nonslip material on it, is the engine-access door, with an air-inlet grille. To the right rear of the driver's cupola is the ventilator-aspirator valve, which provided air to the engine and the cargo compartment when the vehicle was operating on water. Aft of that valve is the air-exhaust grille; farther aft are the cargo-hatch doors, with a center beam between them. *Steve Zaloga collection*

On the rear of the LVTP7 is the ramp, with a personnel door on its left side. At the upper center of the ramp is a vision block, with two vertical guards. A tow cable was stored on the ramp. On the rears of the sponsons are the water-jet deflectors, which directed the water as it was expelled, to steer the vehicle when operating in water. Above each deflector is a taillight assembly. *USMC*

The cargo compartment of the LVTP7, viewed with the ramp lowered, had provisions for seating twenty-four troops, with a folding bench seat on each side and a removable bench seat along the center of the compartment. Here, the seats are stored, as configured when the vehicle was transporting cargo. In the housing in the background are routed the engine exhaust and the air exhaust. To the right of the housing is the station for the vehicle commander, who also was the operator of the armament station. In the left background are, *from rear to front*, the stations for the assistant driver, the troop commander, and the driver.

to protect the mechanicals of the AAV by limiting the engine to idle rpm. The low engine rpm limited the capacity of the bilge pump, and as the vehicle settled, the engine fan splashed water on the generator belt, causing slippage and reduced output. This in turn impaired the operation of the radio system as well as the lighting system in the crew compartment. A broken hatch handle led to a delay in opening an upper rear cargo hatch once the evacuation order was given. Another AAV7A1, having spotted a distress flag, finally reached 523519 but, in doing so, bumped into it, turning the stricken amtrac broadside to the sea. A swell entered through the open rough-top hatch, knocking the fear-laden Marines inside—who were chest deep in water, despite standing on the troop seats—off their feet and disorienting them.

An extensive investigation into this incident followed, including recovery and examination of 523519, and in an effort to prevent a repeat of this tragedy, all AAV7A1s in the Marine Corps were inspected with updated watertight-integrity requirements and bilge pump functionality.

Those inspections found, according to Lt. Gen. Steven Rudder, commander of Marine Forces Pacific, that "a majority of the AAVs failed to meet the new inspection criteria. The leading causes of failure during these inspections were plenum leakage failures, inoperable Emergency Egress Lighting System, and bilge pump discrepancies. Maintaining the reliability of this platform requires

consistent assessment over time to ensure vehicle readiness and safety." According to the February 25, 2021, USMC report on this incident, the doomed AAV7 suffered from these problems, in addition to those already named.

On December 16, 2021, a Marine Corps spokesman, Maj. Jim Stenger, issued the following statement: "The Marine Corps stands by the efficacy of the recommendations that came from the multiple investigations into the AAV mishap from the summer of 2020, and with those recommendations implemented and sustained, the AAV is a safe and effective vehicle for amphibious operations. That said, given the current state of the amphibious-vehicle program [the program that manages both AAVs and ACVs], the commandant of the Marine Corps has decided the AAV will no longer serve as part of regularly scheduled deployments or train in the water during military exercises; AAVs will only return to operating in the water if needed for crisis response. This decision was made in the interest of the long-term health of the amphibious-vehicle programs and future capabilities. The AAV will continue to operate on land; 76 percent of its tasks are land based. In doing so, we reserve the capability to reverse this decision should the need arise."

An upper-right-rear view of an LVTP7 shows the arrangement of the ramp, water-jet deflectors, cargo hatch, cupolas, armament station, and right sponson. On the sloping top of the sponson are a spare-track shoe, pioneer tools, a handrail, the support for the right cargo-hatch door, and grab handles. To the right of the troop commander's hatch is the engine exhaust outlet. *Steve Zaloga collection*

This LVTP7 has been painted in a MERDC camouflage scheme. On the sponson below the driver's hatch is a grab handle, below which is a recessed step/grab handle, both of which were for assisting personnel to climb to the upper deck. *Steve Zaloga collection*

An AAVP7A1 (as the LVTP7A1 was redesignated in 1984: AAVP stands for Amphibious Assault Vehicle, Personnel) parked on a beach has a bow plane, an enhanced appliqué armor kit by Rafael Armor Development Authority, a raised cupola for the troop commander, and a new engine exhaust to the rear of the troop commander's cupola. In 1987 the original armament station was upgraded to the Cadillac Gage Up-Gunned Weapon Station (UGWS), which featured a redesigned turret with a .50-caliber M2 HB machine gun and a Mk. 19 40 mm grenade launcher. *Chris Hughes*

Further details are in view on a Marine Corps AAVP7A1 with enhanced appliqué armor, from 1st Battalion, 23rd Infantry Convoy, during a multinational readiness exercise at Ventspils, Latvia, on June 6, 2017. The .50-caliber machine gun has red paint on it and a yellow device on the muzzle. On the near side is the 40 mm grenade launcher, with a flex chute for ammunition along the side. On the rear of the UGWS are two groups of four smoke-grenade launchers. *Chris Hughes*

An AAVP7A1 creates big waves as it approaches shore. To the front of the troop commander's cupola is a raised periscope, to enable him to see over the driver's cupola. *Chris Hughes*

An elevated view of an AAVP7A1 shows the nonslip materials on the forward deck and engine-compartment access door. Atop the turret of the UGWS is a cupola with vision blocks and a hatch door. Atop the rear part of the sponson are two stops for the cargo-hatch door, a raised support for a radio antenna, and a baggage rack. Since the late 1990s, AAVs have had further upgrades under the Assault Amphibious Vehicle Reliability, Availability, Maintainability / Rebuild to Standard (AAV RAM/RS) Program. Under this program, the AAVs received the Cummins VTA 903 turbosupercharged diesel engine, the new muffler and guard, and a new suspension adapted from that of the US Army M2 Bradley Fighting Vehicle. *Chris Hughes*

Rectangular and square bosses are at intervals on the left sponson of an AAVP7A1 on outdoor display; these were the anchor points for appliqué armor. To the rear of the troop commander's cupola is the muffler, with its curved, steel-mesh guard. An arch-shaped step is on the side skirt. *Chris Hughes*

The display AAVP7A1 features a bow plane, boxy recesses for the headlights, and the angular turret of the Cadillac Gage UGWS, with the .50-caliber machine gun and the 40 mm grenade launcher not installed. *Chris Hughes*

On the rear of the turret bustle is the right bracket for four smoke-grenade launchers; the launchers have been dismounted. A handrail is on the turret base. Lifting rings are on the turret roof, and the top of the cupola is visible. The baggage rack on the sponson was part of the AAV RAM/RS Program improvements. *Chris Hughes*

Details of the design of the turret of the UGWS are viewed from a closer perspective. A series of closely spaced footman loops are welded to the top and the bottom of the side of the turret. *Chris Hughes*

Several bogie wheels and their torsion arms, two track-support rollers, and the track are observed. Work completed on these amtracs as part of the AAV RAM/RS Program included installing new suspension components adapted from similar components on the Bradley Fighting Vehicle. *Chris Hughes*

The idlers installed during AAV RAM/RS upgrades were different from those originally installed on the LVTP7, having six spokes with oblong cutouts between them. *Chris Hughes*

A basic variant of the LVTP7 was the LVTC7 command vehicle, which, with upgrades, including revised headlight locations and a raised cupola and periscope for the troop commander, became the LVTC7A1. Early in production, the command vehicles had the armament station, but later this was deleted and replaced with a cupola with vision blocks. The command vehicles had extra radio sets and antennas and, in addition to the vehicle crew, carried five communications-systems operators and four staff personnel. This LVTC7A1 bears USMC registration no. 397795. *Steve Zaloga collection*

As seen through the ramp opening, the LVTC7A1 had radio sets and five operators' seats on the left side of the cargo compartment, and five seats, a folding staff desk, and a sliding map board on the right side. *Steve Zaloga collection*

A command version of the LVTP7 was produced, the LVTC7, which was succeeded by the improved LVTC7A1 in the early 1980s, as seen here (in 1985, the LVTC7A1 was redesignated AAVC7A1). The vehicle was equipped with additional radio sets and antennas, with stations in the cargo compartment for nine radio operators and staff personnel. Instead of an armament station, the vehicle commander had a cupola with vision blocks and a pan-shaped hatch door. Two supports were furnished for each cargo hatch door. All over the sponsons are bosses for mounting an appliqué armor kit. *Chris Hughes*

This AAVC7A1 is equipped with a hydraulically operated bow plane, which was raised during operations on water, to improve vehicular stability. The -A1 versions of the AAVP7 family of amtracs deleted the original, round recesses for the headlights, substituting two square recesses for the headlights at the top of the bow. Each headlight array included a blackout marker light over a service headlight and an infrared headlight. *Chris Hughes*

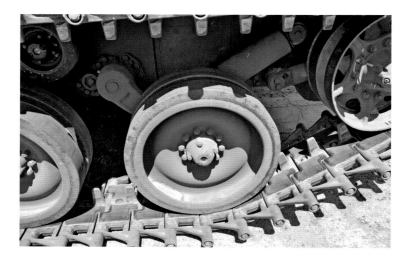

The rear of the suspension on the left side of the AAVC7A1 is shown, including a track-support roller (*upper left*), two of the dual bogie wheels, and the idler (*right*). Originally, the tracks were supported by the tops of the bogie wheels, but the suspension was redesigned under the AAV RAM/RS Program starting in 1997, and three track-support rollers per side were added, which held the tracks above the tops of the bogie wheels. *Chris Hughes*

The right idler is shown close-up; it was six 20 × 3.5. The idlers were equipped with hydraulic track tensioners, which automatically adjusted the positions of the idlers to maintain proper tension in the tracks. *Chris Hughes*

The LVTR7 and the improved LVTR7A1 were designed to serve with the Marine Corps as tracked, amphibious recovery vehicles, with duties such as recovering mired or damaged vehicles, removing and replacing power packs, and general lifting and winching operations. As seen on an LVTR7A1, the vehicle was equipped with a telescoping crane with a tractor seat and controls for the operator on the right side. The crane had a maximum boom capacity of 6,000 pounds. On the rear of the upper deck was a recovery winch with a maximum line-pull rating of 30,000 pounds. On the top of the bow was a fairlead, for routing the winch cable toward the front of the vehicle. *Steve Zaloga collection*

The crane of this LVTR7A1 is directed to the right rear. These vehicles had a cupola with vision blocks and a hatch door instead of an armament station. The LVTR7 and LVTR7A1 could tow vehicles up to their own weight on land or water. The LVTR7A1 WAS redesignated AAVR7A1 in 1985. *Steve Zaloga collection*

A display LVTR7 lacks the fairlead assembly atop the bow. Visible below the crane boom is the hydraulic cylinder. Toward the rear of the sponson is the support for the boom. *Chris Hughes*

The headlights are in the round recesses, a hallmark of the LVTR7; the LVTR7A1/AAVR7A1 had square recesses for the headlights at the top of the bow. The headlight lenses have been painted over. The towing ring between the headlights was a feature of the LVTR7 but not of the LVTP7. *Chris Hughes*

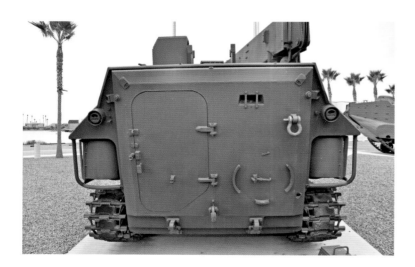

The recovery winch has been removed from the rear of the upper deck, but parts of its mounting remain in place. Otherwise, the features on the rear of the LVTR7 were identical to those of the LVTP7. *Chris Hughes*

The end of the boom of the crane is viewed close-up, with the steel ball for the hook below it. Also in view is the support, which cradled the boom during travel. *Chris Hughes*

The boom of the LVTR7 is viewed from the right rear of the LVTR7. The footman loops on the sponson were for securing the pioneer tools. *Chris Hughes*

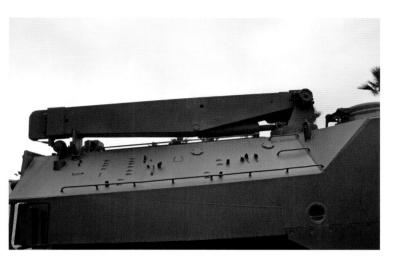

The full length of the crane is viewed from the right side of the vehicle. Below the boom are the hydraulic cylinder and piston. Mounted on the sponson in line with the turret is the doorstop for the cupola hatch. *Chris Hughes*

The left side of the crane turret is seen from the right side of the LVTR7. Mounted on the upper part of the turret is the winch for the hoist cable, manufactured by Tulsa Winch Company. *Chris Hughes*

The winch operator's seat and controls have been removed from the right side of the crane. The water-jet deflectors on the rears of the sponsons have tubular guards. The water intakes for the jets are on the undersides of the sponsons. *Chris Hughes*

The preserved LVTR7, minus the prominent fairlead atop the bow, the crane operator's station, and the recovery winch, is seen from the left front. *Chris Hughes*

FMC produced two prototype LVTEX3 engineer amtracs during 1970. The vehicle featured a front dozer blade and provisions for three rocket-propelled explosive line charges, for clearing minefields and obstructions. An armament station was installed. Later, the two LVTEX3s received improvements to bring them up to production standard, and they were redesignated LVTE7. However, the project was canceled before series production began. One of the LVTE7s is shown with the rocket launchers deployed. *Steve Zaloga collection*

The LVTP7s first entered service in early April 1972, with the 2nd Amphibian Tractor (Amtrac) Battalion, 2nd Marine Division, at Camp Lejeune, North Carolina. A few weeks later, on April 19, two LVTP7s from Company B, 2nd Amphibian Tractor Battalion, have landed on Onslow Beach at Lejeune. The vehicle on the left is marked B05, and the one to the right B34. The armament stations lack the machine guns.

Marines from Company C, 2nd Recon Battalion, 2nd Marine Division, are disembarking from the same two LVTP7s in the preceding photo, B05 and B34, during a training exercise at Onslow Beach on April 19, 1972. The semicircular hatch doors of the armament stations are in view.

Six LVTP7s from 1st Platoon, Company B, 2nd Amtrac Battalion, are proceeding along Onslow Beach during a field exercise named Exotic Dancer at Camp Lejeune on May 18, 1972. The lead vehicle is marked "B47."

Company A, 1st Amtrac Battalion, 3rd Marine Division, was equipped with LVTP7s. Marines are hitting the beach from a pair of LVTP7s during a field-training exercise at Camp Schwab, Okinawa, on May 18, 1973. The vehicle to the left is marked "1-Y-10" on the bow and the side of the hull, while the amtrac to the right is "1-Y-13."

LVTP7s from the 2nd Amphibious Tractor Battalion, Force Troops, are filing ashore during a training exercise at New River, North Carolina, on June 5, 1975. On the second vehicle in the column, a spotlight on a pedestal has been mounted on the front of the armament station.

AAVP7A1s (as LVTP7A1s recently had been redesignated) are laying down a smokescreen as they come ashore during Exercise Bright Star '87, an annual/semiannual joint US-Egyptian training exercise first held in December 1980. The AAVP7A1 was equipped to generate smoke by introducing fuel into the exhaust system.

The driver of an AAVP7A1 painted in a woodland MERDC camouflage pattern is awaiting orders to move forward at Naval Station Roosevelt Roads, Puerto Rico, during Ocean Venture '88. This joint US Marine Corps, Navy, and Army training and readiness exercise was held from April 1 to 22, 1988, and included the 6th Marine Brigade, from Camp Lejeune, North Carolina. The smoke-grenade launchers of the Up-Gunned Weapon Station (UGWS) are in view. To the front of the driver's hatch door is the ventilator-aspirator valve, which supplied air to the engine when the vehicle was afloat.

Two Marines are going over their checklists in an AAVC7A1 command amtrac during exercise Ocean Venture '88. The cargo hatch doors above are open, with the central beam dividing the halves of the hatch. In the right foreground are three 5-gallon liquid containers.

During an amphibious warfare demonstration during the 14th Annual Inter-American Naval Conference in May 1988, Marines have debarked from an AAVP7A1 at Naval Air Base Little Creek, Virginia. The MERDC-camouflaged amtrac has the UGWS.

In a companion view to the preceding photo, an AAVP7A1 is escorting Marines as they advance up a beach at NAB Little Creek in May 1988. In the right background is a Newport-class landing ship, tank (LST), which served as a transport for amphibious craft.

A group of Marines pose next to a row of AAVP7A1s during the 14th Annual Inter-American Naval Conference at NAB Little Creek in May 1988. The first two amtracs have the UGWS, with the angular turret, while the third amtrac has the early-type armament station, with vision blocks around the turret.

Two Marine AAVP7A1s have landed at Pattaya Beach, Thailand, during the joint Thai/US Exercise Thalay Thai '89 in September 1988. The lead vehicle bears registration no. 522975. Both of the armament stations are the early type and have been modified with two four-tube smoke-grenade launchers.

A convoy of Marine Corps AAVP-7 amphibious assault vehicles halt along a coastal road in Alaska during Exercise Pacex '89, a joint US-Japanese navy exercise in the Pacific in September 1989. The amtracs exhibit both the early-type armament stations and the later, angular UGWS turrets.

An AAVR7A1 amphibious recovery vehicle, *left*, and three AAVP7A1 amphibious assault vehicles have just landed on a beach during the joint service exercise Ocean Venture '90, in January 1990. The AAVR7A1's crane is visible, as are the fairlead atop the bow and the distinctive towing eye on the front of the bow.

A Marine Corps AAVP7A1 is deployed in Saudi Arabia during Operation Desert Shield, the operation in preparation for the military offensive against Iraqi occupation forces in Kuwait, in January 1990. The vehicle is painted in a MERDC desert camouflage scheme. Just beyond this vehicle is another AAVP71, the top and several occupants of which are visible.

An evidently nonstandard equipment rack is on the sponson of this Marine Corps AAVP7A1, approaching a beach in Rayong Province, Thailand, during the combined Thai/US exercise Cobra Gold '90, in June 1990. Bosses for attaching appliqué armor are on the side of the hull.

Two Marine Corps AAVP-7A1 amphibious assault vehicles painted in desert camouflage are advancing through a desert in Kuwait after the Iraqi retreat from that country during Operation Desert Storm, in February 1991. In this offensive campaign, Marine amtracs conducted diversionary landings, transported Marines, and performed engineer service. The 2nd, 3rd, and 4th Assault Amphibian Battalions operated amtracs in Desert Storm.

Although the LVTE7 engineer amtrac, with its ability to launch line charges to clear minefields by blowing them up, did not enter series production, the Mk. 154 mine-clearance kit was available to give the AAVP71 that capability. These Marines from the 2nd Combat Engineer Battalion, 2nd Marine Division, and assigned to Task Force Breach Alpha, are installing a Mk. 154 kit on an AAVP7A1 at a base in Saudi Arabia during Operation Desert Storm. The installation included a low superstructure with hatch doors over the original cargo hatch. On the rear of the superstructure are two brackets, which will support a rack with three rockets, which propel the M59 line charges. A large container is yet to be installed in the cargo compartment, to hold the line charges. The AAVP7A1 could fire line charges on land as well as while afloat, to detonate submerged mines.

A Marine Corps AAVP7A1 amphibious assault vehicle, marked D-31 and bearing chevron-shaped recognition symbols, is advancing past an abandoned Iraqi strongpoint during the ground phase of Operation Desert Storm. A large amount of packs, baggage, and other equipment is stored on the vehicle. The turret is the early type, with vision blocks and an M85 12.7 mm machine gun.

General Data	
Model	AAV7A1
Weight*	56,552
Length**	321.3
Width**	128.7
Height**	130.5
Max speed, land/water	30 mph / 6 mph
Fuel capacity	171 gal.
Range	300 miles
Range land	300 miles
Engine Data	
Engine make/model	Cummins VT400
Number of cylinders	8 90-degree V
Cubic-inch displacement	903

* Fighting weight, in pounds
** Overall dimensions listed in inches

"POINT MASTER" is the nickname assigned to AAVP7A1 registration no. 523352, serving with the 2nd Marine Expeditionary Force during the ground phase of Operation Desert Storm, Kuwait. The UGWS is viewed from the right rear; above the front of the turret is a small spotlight. A pair of binoculars is resting atop the periscope housing.

With the Lincoln Memorial in the background, an AAVP7A1 marked simply "US MARINES" on the bow and the side of the hull is participating in the National Victory Celebration parade, a daylong celebration honoring the Coalition's victory over Iraq in Operation Desert Storm, on June 8, 1991.

Marine AAVP7A1s participated in Operation Restore Hope, a 1992–93 US-led, multination peacekeeping and aid mission to civil-war-torn Somalia. Here, a beachmaster directs two AAVP7A1s from the 3rd Assault Amphibian Battalion at the international airport at Mogadishu, Somalia, in December 1992. The battalion had landed at Mogadishu on December 9. Both amtracs have the enhanced appliqué armor kit (EAAK), produced by Rafael Armament Development Authority, of Israel.

Members of the 22nd Marine Expeditionary Unit (Special Operations Capable) egress from an AAVP7A1 during the first major US-Kuwaiti joint training exercise since the end of Operation Desert Storm, in a desert in Kuwait in March 1993. Two vehicle crewmen wearing body armor and CVC helmets wired into the intercom system are standing by the ramp. Inside is a red-and-white civilian-type cooler.

Five AAVP7A1s are rolling past a battery of concealed M198 155 mm howitzers of Battery R, 5th Battalion, 10th Marines, during the joint service exercise Ocean Venture '93, on Vieques Island, Puerto Rico, in May 1993. All the amtracs are equipped with EAAK protection.

Elements of a Marine Corps tank company have come ashore on dare, preparing to breach obstacles during Exercise Kernel Blitz, at Red Beach, Camp Pendleton, California, in April 1999. *From left to right*, an M9 armored combat earthmover (ACE), an Abrams M1A1 main battle tank with the M1 mine-clearing blade system, and an AAVP7A1. The amtrac has the UGWS and the EAAK.

A photographer aboard the amphibious assault ship USS *Bataan* (LHD-5) took a very informative photo of this AAV7A1, registration no. 522613, approaching the ship during an amphibious training exercise on May 18, 2013. The vehicle was assigned to the 2nd Assault Amphibian Battalion, 2nd Marine Division. The bow plane has been deployed, and a tow cable is attached to clevises and a handrail on the forward deck. A small spotlight is mounted on a pedestal on the sleeve for the M2 HB machine gun of the UGWS. A flexible ammunition chute is routed from the left side of the turret to the 40 mm grenade launcher. Appliqué armor panels on the cargo-hatch doors and the center beam of the hatch were part of the EAAK protection. The baggage racks and the radio-antenna supports on the aft parts of the sponson are of a matte black or dark-gray color.

A USMC AAV7A1 assault amphibious vehicle from Headquarters and Service Company, 3rd Assault Amphibious Battalion, 1st Marine Division, is negotiating a ten-bay, medium-girder bridge during a training exercise at Camp Pendleton, California, on December 4, 2013. On this amtrac, the baggage rack and antenna supports have been painted green, to match the surrounding camouflage paint. The upgraded suspension, including new bogie wheels, track-support rollers, and idlers, introduced with the RAM/RS Program, are in view.

Another AAV7A1 from Headquarters and Service Company, 3rd Assault Amphibious Battalion, is crossing the engineer bridge at Camp Pendleton on December 4, 2013. The bridge was emplaced by the Bridge Company, 7th Engineer Support Battalion, 1st Marine Logistics Group, as part of that battalion's readiness training.

An AAV7A1, registration no. 5322649, and crew are proceeding up a ramp at Camp Lejeune, North Carolina, following a demonstration of the vehicle's capabilities to US Navy midshipmen during a Career Orientation for Midshipmen (CORTAMID) session, on July 28, 2015. Standing by to the right is another AAV7A1, registration no. 523567.

A Marine from Bravo Company, 1st Combat Engineer Battalion (1st CEB), is exiting an AAV7A1 through the personnel door in the ramp during Exercise Pioneer Express at the US Army National Guard base at Camp Roberts, California, on September 1, 2015. The left cargo-hatch door is open and is resting on the supports. The tubular guards for the water-jet deflectors, present on the LVTP7 and LVTP71, had been deleted.

A USMC AAV7A1 from the 13th Marine Expeditionary Unit is participating in an amphibious assault drill during exercise Ssang Yong '16 in the Republic of Korea on March 12, 2016. Participating in this biennial, multinational amphibious exercise are US forces, the Republic of Korea Navy and Marine Corps, the Australian Army, and the Royal New Zealand Army. Six plastic liquid containers are secured to the upper deck to the rear of the UGWS, and a rusted bogie wheel is in the baggage rack on the sponson.

AAV7A1s from the 22nd Marine Expeditionary Unit are spotted on the well deck of the dock landing ship USS *Whidbey Island* (LSD-41) in readiness for an upcoming exercise, on March 18, 2016. The basic vehicles are painted in three-color NATO camouflage, but the enhanced appliqué armor is painted solely in green. The fasteners that hold the appliqué sections in place are bright metal.

AAV7A1s assigned to the 2nd Assault Amphibian Battalion, 2nd Marine Division, are being readied to start an amphibious movement during a Marine Corps Combat Readiness Evaluation (MCCRE) at Camp Lejeune, North Carolina, on October 24, 2016. The UGWSs on the amtracs are fitted with dustcovers over the fronts, which also include sleeves for the .50-caliber and 40 mm barrels. The closest vehicle bears registration no. 523380 on the front of the bow.

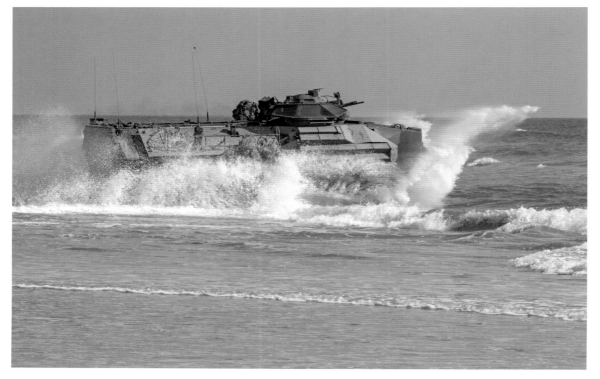

As part of a mechanized boat-raid course at Marine Corps Base Camp Pendleton, California, members of 1st Battalion, 5th Marines, 1st Marine Division, are being transported in an AAV7A1 from the shore to a ship. This course prepares Marines for duty with the motorized raid force of the 31st Marine Expeditionary Unit.